Bloom's
GUIDES

William Shakespeare's
Romeo and Juliet

CURRENTLY AVAILABLE

1984
The Adventures of Huckleberry Finn
All the Pretty Horses
Beloved
Brave New World
The Chosen
The Crucible
Cry, the Beloved Country
Death of a Salesman
The Grapes of Wrath
Great Expectations
Hamlet
The Handmaid's Tale
The House on Mango Street
I Know Why the Caged Bird Sings
The Iliad
Lord of the Flies
Macbeth
Maggie: A Girl of the Streets
The Member of the Wedding
Pride and Prejudice
Ragtime
Romeo and Juliet
The Scarlet Letter
Snow Falling on Cedars
A Streetcar Named Desire
The Things They Carried
To Kill a Mockingbird

Bloom's
GUIDES

William Shakespeare's
Romeo
and Juliet

Edited & with an Introduction
by Harold Bloom

CHELSEA HOUSE
PUBLISHERS
A Haights Cross Communications Company
Philadelphia

Contributing editor: Neil Heims
Cover design by Takeshi Takahashi
Layout by EJB Publishing Services

First Printing
1 3 5 7 9 8 6 4 2

Romeo and Juliet / [edited by] Harold Bloom.
    p. cm. — (Bloom's guides)
  Includes bibliographical references.
  ISBN 0-7910-8170-2 (alk. paper)
  1. Shakespeare, William, 1564-1616. Romeo and Juliet. I. Bloom,
Harold. II. Series.
  PR2831.R636 2005
  822.3'3—dc22
                                    2004027464

Contents

# Introduction

HAROLD BLOOM

Harold C. Goddard, in his *The Meaning of Shakespeare* (1951), remarked upon how much of Shakespeare turns upon the vexed relationships between generations of the same family, which was also one of the burdens of Athenian tragedy. Except for the early *Titus Andronicus*, which I judge to have been a charnel-house parody of Christopher Marlowe, *Romeo and Juliet* was Shakespeare's first venture at composing a tragedy, and also his first deep investigation of generational perplexities. The Montague–Capulet hatred might seem overwrought enough to have its parodistic aspects, but it destroys two immensely valuable, very young lovers, Juliet of the Capulets and Romeo of the Montagues, and Mercutio as well, a far more interesting character than Romeo. Yet Romeo, exalted by the authentic love between the even more vital Juliet and himself, is one of the first instances of the Shakespearean representation of crucial change in a character through self-overhearing and self-reflection. Juliet, an even larger instance, is the play's triumph, since she inaugurates Shakespeare's extraordinary procession of vibrant, life-enhancing women, never matched before or since in all of Western literature, including in Chaucer, who was Shakespeare's truest precursor as the creator of personalities.

Juliet, Mercutio, the nurse, and to a lesser extent Romeo are among the first Shakespearean characters who manifest their author's uncanny genius at inventing persons. Richard III, like Aaron the Moor in *Titus Andronicus*, is a brilliant Marlovian cartoon or grotesque, but lacks all inwardness, which is true also of the figures in the earliest comedies. Faulconbridge the Bastard in *King John* and Richard II were Shakespeare's initial breakthroughs in the forging of personalities, before the composition of *Romeo and Juliet*. After Juliet, Mercutio, and the nurse came Bottom, Shylock, Portia, and most overwhelmingly Falstaff, with whom at last Shakespeare was fully himself.

Harold Goddard shrewdly points out that the nurse, who lacks wit, imagination, and above all love, even for Juliet, is no Falstaff, who abounds in cognitive power, creative humor, and (alas) love for the undeserving Hal. The nurse is ferociously lively and funny, but she proves to be exactly what the supremely accurate Juliet eventually calls her: "most wicked fiend," whose care for Juliet has no inward reality. In some sense, the agent of Juliet's tragedy is the nurse, whose failure in loving the child she has raised leads Juliet to the desperate expedient that destroys both Romeo and herself.

Mercutio, a superb and delightful role, nevertheless is inwardly quite as cold as the nurse. Though he is Shakespeare's first sketch of a charismatic individual (Berowne in *Love's Labor's Lost* has brilliant language, but no charisma), Mercutio is a dangerous companion for Romeo, and becomes redundant as soon as Romeo passes from sexual infatuation to sincere love, from Rosaline to Juliet. Age-old directorial wisdom is that Shakespeare killed off Mercutio so quickly, because Romeo is a mere stick in contrast to his exuberant friend. But Mercutio becomes irrelevant once Juliet and Romeo fall profoundly in love with one another. What place has Mercutio in the play once it becomes dominated by Juliet's magnificent avowal of her love's infinitude:

> And yet I wish but for the thing I have.
> My bounty is as boundless as the sea,
> My love as deep; the more I give to thee,
> The more I have, for both are infinite.

Contrast that with Mercutio at his usual bawdry:

> If love be blind, love cannot hit the mark.
> Now will he sit under a medlar tree,
> And wish his mistress were that kind of fruit
> As maids call medlars, when they laugh alone.
> O, Romeo, that she were, O that she were
> An open-arse, thou a pu'rin pear!

Since Juliet develops from strength to strength, Romeo (who is only partly a convert to love) is inevitably dwarfed by her. Partly this is the consequence of what will be Shakespeare's long career of comparing women to men to men's accurate disadvantage, a career that can be said to commence with precisely this play. But partly the tragic flaw is in Romeo himself, who yields too readily to many fierce emotions: anger, fear, grief, and despair. This yielding leads to the death of Tybalt, to Romeo's own suicide, and to Juliet's own farewell to life. Shakespeare is careful to make Romeo just as culpable, in his way, as Mercutio or Tybalt. Juliet, in total contrast, remains radically free of flaw: she is a saint of love, courageous and trusting, refusing the nurse's evil counsel and attempting to hold on to love's truth, which she incarnates. Though it is "The Tragedy of Romeo and Juliet," the lovers are tragic in wholly different ways. Juliet, in a curious prophecy of Hamlet's charismatic elevation, transcends her self-destruction and dies exalted. Romeo, not of her eminence, dies more pathetically. We are moved by both deaths, but Shakespeare sees to it that our larger loss is the loss of Juliet.

Biographical Sketch

Although there is a great deal of documentary material (baptismal certificates, marriage licenses, property deeds, mortgages, accounts of law suits, death certificates, a will, etc.), of Shakespeare's actual life little is really known. Whether the man identified as the author of the body of work called Shakespeare's even was the Shakespeare who wrote those works is a question still debated by some.

Shakespeare was baptized on April 26, 1564, in Stratford-on-Avon in England. Traditionally, April 23rd is held to be his birthday, for it is St. George's day (St. George is England's patron saint) and Shakespeare died on April 23rd in 1616. Shakespeare's father, John Shakespeare was a tanner and a glover: he cured animal hides and made them into leather goods like gloves and purses. He was the son of a tenant farmer, Richard Shakespeare, who lived four miles northeast of Stratford in the village of Snitterfield, working for a wealthy landowner, Robert Arden. John Shakespeare married Robert Arden's daughter Mary, and she brought considerable wealth to him. During his first years in Stratford, John Shakespeare grew prosperous and served the town in a number of elected offices including as ale-taster, alderman, and high bailiff, or mayor. In 1570, he applied for a coat-of-arms and for the privilege of writing "Gentleman" after his name. But soon after—it is not known why—his fortune and his public reputation took a turn for the worse. He withdrew his application. In 1580, he had to mortgage his wife's property to pay debts; of the three houses he had once owned, now only one still belonged to him. His name later appears on public records when he was fined for not attending council sessions, not appearing in court, and not attending church.

William Shakespeare was the third of John and Mary's children, but the first to survive childhood. He had two brothers, Gilbert, an actor, and Edmund, a haberdasher, who grew into adulthood, although each died rather young. He gave Gilbert a splendid funeral. His sister Joan lived to be seventy-seven and two of her daughters lived into adulthood and married.

Shakespeare probably went to the Stratford Grammar School. Since his father was an alderman, his tuition would have been waived. According to Nicholas Rowe, his first biographer, writing in 1709, he was withdrawn from school in 1678, in order to work, when his father's fortunes began to slide. There are no records regarding Shakespeare again until November 1682 when his marriage to Anne Hathaway is recorded in the church register in Stratford. The name Hathwey appears on the second entry. Anne Whateley is the name written down when the license is first issued. What is probably an error on the part of an inattentive clerk (the name Whateley appears elsewhere on the same page with regard to other business) has become grounds for much fanciful speculation about Shakespeare's love life.

Anne Hathaway was twenty-six and several months pregnant when they married. She and William settled in his father's house on Henley Street in Stratford. Their first child, Susanna, was christened May 26, 1583. In January 1585, twins, Hamnet and Judith, were born. Hamnet died at the age of eleven in 1596. Judith and Susanna lived into adulthood, married and had children.

The years between 1585 and 1592 are unaccounted for. It is likely, however, although it cannot be substantiated, that Shakespeare went to London around 1587 with one of the troupes of traveling players that passed through the villages of England. Shakespeare comes back into historical view at the end of 1592 when reference is made to him as a force on the London theater scene by the dramatist Robert Greene in his autobiography *A Groatsworth of Wit*. Greene calls Shakespeare "an upstart crow" who "is as well able to bombast out a blank verse as the best of you," and that "being an absolute Johannes Factotum, is in his own conceit the only Shake-scene in a country." Greene's insult not only reintroduces Shakespeare to the record, but served at the time to elicit more information about him. Henry Chettle, who had edited Greene's papers, later, apologized, in the Preface to his *Kind-Heart's Dream*, for printing Greene's remark. He wrote of Shakespeare that he had personal acquaintance with him and had "seen his demeanor no less civil than he excellent in the quality he professes." Furthermore, Chettle spoke of Shakespeare's "uprightness of dealing, which argues his honesty," and of "his ... grace in writing."

By 1591 Shakespeare's name was known on the London stage. His *Henry VI* plays had been performed by *The Admiral's Company*. In the summer of 1592, however, London theaters were closed because of the plague. During this period Shakespeare wrote *Venus and Adonis*, the early sonnets, and *The Rape of Lucrece*. When the theaters reopened in 1594, Shakespeare had joined with several other notable actors of the time, Richard Burbage, John Heminge, Will Kempe, and Henry Condell, to form *The Lord Chamberlain's Men*. They became the foremost company of the time, performed at the Globe Theater, an outdoor theater, and the Blackfriars, a more exclusive indoor house. They also performed at court for Queen Elizabeth. In 1596, Shakespeare reinstated his father's appeal for a coat-of-arms, and it was granted. He had a house, New Place, built in Stratford. With the ascendancy of James I, *The Lord Chamberlain's Men* became *His Majesty's Servants, the King's Men*. Shakespeare and his fellow actors became Grooms of the Chamber, and their revenues increased too, for James demanded many more court performances than had Elizabeth. Beside his career in the theater Shakespeare made several real estate investments in London.

Shakespeare was forty-six when he went into semi-retirement. He returned to Stratford, but did not stop writing for the London stage and probably traveled between the two towns frequently. At the age of fifty-two he died of what seemed to be a sudden illness. Not long before, he had drawn up his will, bequeathing most of his wealth to his two daughters. We know nothing of his relationship with or his feelings about his wife, Anne. The only bequest he made to her in his will has become famous for its odd and puzzling character. He left her his "second best bed." Perhaps there is no puzzle, however; our best bed is the grave, which affords the truest rest. Any bed in life, compared to that one can be only second best. On the vault of the church over his tomb, Shakespeare had inscribed a plea not to disturb his bones by exhumation.

In 1623, seven years after Shakespeare's death, members of his acting company collected the manuscripts of his plays and printed them in one volume, *The First Folio*. Within its pages the scanty narrative of Shakespeare's temporal and outer life gives way to the overwhelmingly rich narrative of an inner life that has created for Shakespeare an endless being.

The Story Behind the Story

When *Romeo and Juliet* was first published in 1597, the title page of what is now called the first Quarto, described it as having been "often (with great applause) plaid publiquely, by the right Ho-/nourable the L. Hunsdon his servants." (Lord Hundson was Queen Elizabeth's Lord Chamberlain and the patron of Shakespeare's acting company.) This allows us to date the composition of the play at around 1595 or 1596. There was no author credited, however. The first attribution of the play to Shakespeare can be found in a 1598 diary entry by a London theatergoer named Francis Meres. The first Quarto is a corrupt text, not copied from Shakespeare's manuscript, but a memorial reconstruction of the play provided to the printer by one of the actors who had performed in it. In 1599, a second Quarto was published. The title page states that it is *"Newly corrected, augmented, and amended."* It is a far better text, taken from a manuscript close to Shakespeare's original, and it is the one upon which all succeeding editions of the play have been based, including the 1623 Folio edition. (A quarto is a volume whose pages are made by folding the paper on which it is printed in four. For a folio, the paper is folded in half.)

The story of Romeo and Juliet was well-known in Elizabethan England, and by the time of Shakespeare's play it had appeared in several collections and in several forms. There were versions in two Elizabethan compendia with which Shakespeare was familiar, Belleforest's *Histoires Tragiques* and William Painter's *Palace of Pleasure*. Scholars believe that Shakespeare's primary source, however, is a long poem by Arthur Brooke called *The Tragical Historye of Romeus and Juliet* printed in 1562 and reissued in 1587. In the introduction to his poem, Brooke himself mentions recently having seen "the same argument recently set foorth on the stage." In giving the earlier sources of Shakespeare's *Romeo and Juliet*, then, we must realize that they came to him in all likelihood through Brooke's poem.

The story of two lovers resembling Romeo and Juliet, or

containing elements of a story similar to theirs, was long a part of continental European literature before it crossed over to England. It has analogs in the stories of Dido and Aeneas, Pyramus and Thisbe, and Troilus and Cressida, all sets of lovers whose love is undermined by the social conflicts swirling around them. In the fifth century A.D. narrative, *Ephesiaca*, Xenophon of Ephesus told the story of a wife separated from her husband who avoided marriage to another man by taking a sleeping potion. She, too, awakens in a tomb. In 1476, Masuccio used this motif in a story called *Il Novellino* about Mariotto and Gianozza. They are secretly married by a friar, and Mariotto is exiled after killing someone. Giannozza's father, unaware of his daughter's marriage, plans to marry her to a man of his choosing, and she takes a sleeping potion, escapes from the tomb where she has been interred and goes to Alexandria, where Mariotto lives in banishment. She is preceded by (the false) news of her death. The messenger to Mariotto who was to tell him of her scheme and of her impending arrival has been captured and killed by pirates. Mariotto goes to her tomb, is caught and beheaded. Giannozza dies in a convent.

In 1530 Luigi da Porto took this story as the basis for his *Historia novellamente ritrovata di due Nobili Amanti*. He set it in Verona and introduced the two feuding families, the Montecchi and the Cappelletti. The lovers are called Romeo and Giulietta. When they meet at a Carnival ball, he is suffering from unrequited love, just as Shakespeare's Romeo is. There is no sleeping potion in this version. When Romeo goes to her window to woo her, he mistakes Giulietta asleep for Giulietta dead and kills himself. When she wakes and finds him dead she kills herself *by holding her breath*, an element of the story which, fortunately, did not survive this version. Although there is none of the character development that can be found in Shakespeare, a character named Marcuccio, the prototype for Mercutio, is introduced.

In 1554, Matteo Bandello used Da Porto's novel as the basis for his own rendition of the story, and five years later, in 1559, Pierre Boaistua translated Bandello's version into French in his

Histoire Tragiques. From this rendition of the story, Brooke made his long poem, which is the immediate source of Shakespeare's play.

List of Characters

Romeo is the son of the house of Montague, a wealthy Verona family, and is a young, romantic man. He seems relatively uninvolved in the feud between his family and the Capulets, another wealthy family in the city, and in the course of the play he falls deeply in love with the Capulets' daughter, Juliet. They secretly marry, but events cause Romeo to kill her cousin, Tybalt, and be exiled from the city. Upon hearing a false account of Juliet's death, Romeo goes to her tomb and poisons himself.

Juliet is the daughter of the house of Capulet, which is engaged in a bloody feud with Romeo's family, the Montagues. Juliet, who at the beginning of the play seems merely a young, naive, and obedient daughter, falls in love with Romeo and marries him. She reveals herself to be tough-minded and courageous when her secret marriage with Romeo is threatened by her father's decision to marry her to Paris. She eventually participates in an elaborate plan to avoid the second marriage by feigning her own death. The plan backfires when Romeo, believing her dead, commits suicide; upon discovering his corpse, Juliet fatally stabs herself.

Friar Laurence, a Franciscan monk, performs the secret wedding of Romeo and Juliet and devises the scheme by which Juliet attempts to avoid marrying Paris. The friar is a learned man and offers generally wise advice to a number of other characters; however, the scheme he proposes to Juliet eventually leads to her death, and the deaths of Paris and Romeo.

Juliet's Nurse is a dedicated and loyal, if somewhat empty-headed, ally of Juliet and plays an important role in getting Romeo and Juliet secretly married. Her lack of moral center causes Juliet to discard her as a confidante when she suggests that Juliet marry Paris despite her existing marriage to Romeo because Paris is richer.

Paris, kin to Prince Escalus and Mercutio, is a wealthy nobleman who wishes to marry Juliet. Although he seems a decent man, he is blind to the fact that Juliet does not care for him and does not want to marry him. He is eventually killed by Romeo, whom he attacks when he thinks Romeo is breaking into the Capulet tomb to defile the bodies.

Old Capulet is the head of the Capulet household and Juliet's father. He condones the feud with the Montagues but displays a certain restraint when he prevents Tybalt from attacking Romeo at a party. His character becomes less sympathetic, however, when he attempts to force Juliet to marry the wealthy and powerful Paris. After Romeo and Juliet's suicides, he swears friendship with old Montague.

Tybalt, the nephew of Juliet's mother, is an extremely violent and pugnacious young man who kills Romeo's friend Mercutio and is in turn killed by Romeo, causing Romeo to be exiled from Verona.

Mercutio is a witty and punning young nobleman and kin to both Paris and Prince Escalus. Although he is not a Montague, he takes their side in the feud, an attitude that causes him to challenge Tybalt, who kills him.

Benvolio, the nephew of old Montague, is a calm and reasonable character who attempts to keep the peace in Verona in the face of an escalating feud.

Prince Escalus is the ruler of Verona who exiles Romeo in an attempt to end the Capulet–Montague feud, which he feels is a disturbance and a menace to the citizens of his city.

Lady Capulet, Juliet's mother and Tybalt's aunt, encourages Juliet to marry Paris but objects to her husband's abusive behavior when her daughter refuses.

Old Montague is head of the Montague household and Romeo's father. He obviously cares for his son but encourages the feud that results in his banishment, which causes Lady Montague to die from grief and ultimately leads to Romeo's suicide.

Summary and Analysis

I. Conflicts of Will

On the morning of her wedding day to the County Paris, her father's choice of a husband for her, after Juliet's apparently lifeless body is discovered by her nurse, Friar Laurence offers this consolation:

> She's not well married that lives married long,
> But she's best married that dies married young.
>
> IV.v.77f1

This is awfully peculiar consolation to give to the parents of a girl who has just died. If it means anything at all, it seems to be an implicit criticism of the institution of marriage and the effect that marriage can have on love. A short marriage, by implication, is better than a long one—perhaps because then the passion of love is frozen in eternity rather than transformed into domesticity. Whether true or not as a critique of marriage or an analysis of love, Friar Laurence's words seem singularly irrelevant under the circumstances.

But Friar Laurence is not actually offering the grieving parents, the bereft bridegroom, and the devoted nurse consolation. And the circumstances are different from what they appear to be to Juliet's mourners. Laurence is only giving the appearance of offering consolation. He is actually scolding them, reproaching them, as the opening lines of his speech clearly show, when he interrupts their keening over Juliet's body:

> Peace ho, for shame! Confusion's [cure] lives not
> In these confusions. Heaven and yourself
> Had part in this fair maid, now heaven hath all,
> And all the better it is for the maid.
>
> IV.v.65ff

Even as Friar Laurence warns against confusion, he is doing his best to maintain their confusion in order to make sure that a scheme which he has devised will both remain hidden and will succeed. He is in league with Juliet to thwart her marriage to Paris and to reunite her with Romeo, already her husband. (Juliet is not, in fact dead. She has taken a potion the friar has distilled. Its effect is to simulate the appearance of death for twenty-four hours. After Juliet has been interred, Laurence intends for Romeo, secretly returned from banishment in Mantua, to meet her at the tomb and for the lovers, whom he has clandestinely married, to flee together to safety.) In consequence, his homily is full of deception. It is all the better for Juliet, as far as he is truly concerned, to be married to Romeo rather than to be in heaven, as he implies she is, or to be married to Paris, as her parents wish her to be. This is his real and buried meaning.

Laurence scolds the mourners, using conventional Elizabethan rhetoric, for grieving over her death when he argues,

> The most you sought was her promotion,
> For 'twas your heaven she should be advanc'd,
> And weep ye now, seeing she is advanc'd
> Above the clouds, as high as heaven itself?
> O, is this love, you love your child so ill
> That you run mad, seeing that she is well.
>
> IV.v.71ff

This is a common consolation/admonition, often found in Shakespeare's plays (and often, too, spoken in bad faith, as when Claudius, in *Hamlet*, advises Hamlet that his grief for his dead father is excessive, unnatural, and an insult to heaven). Elizabethans said of the dead that they are well. After all, they are in heaven. It is we who are still on earth, alive and subject therefore to mortal suffering, who are ill. But Juliet is not dead and her parents are grieving and therefore Friar Laurence is deceiving them on two counts; not only is she already married to someone other than Paris, she is not, in Laurence's Elizabethan usage, well, either, since she actually is alive and in the midst of peril largely of their making. And when he sermonizes that "She's not well married that lives married long,/ But she's best married that dies married young," not only is this a false consolation, but, unbeknownst to him, it is ironically prescient, for that will indeed soon be Juliet's fortune. In addition, he is guilty of the "chopped logic" which not long before in stage time had so infuriated Juliet's father.

When Lady Capulet tells Juliet in act 3, scene 5, line 113 that her father has arranged for her to marry Paris, Juliet responds that she "will not marry yet," and continues with an ironic and deceitful equivocation saying, "when I do, I swear/ It shall be to Romeo, whom you know I hate,/ Rather than Paris." Lady Capulet's "knowledge" is not founded on Juliet's testimony but on her own supposition. Romeo has killed Juliet's cousin, Tybalt, the play's marplot, and for that reason Romeo has been banished. Romeo's banishment is the cause of Juliet's grief. Since her parents are unaware of their daughter's love for Romeo, however, and of their marriage, which Friar Laurence performed the previous day—on the morning of the afternoon that Romeo killed Tybalt, in fact—they reasonably attribute her grief to Tybalt's death and assume that she hates Romeo for killing him. A few lines later, after Lady Capulet has told her husband that Juliet will not consent to marry Paris, Capulet explodes in a series of angry questions:

> Soft, take me with you, take me with you, wife.
> How, will she none? Doth she not give us thanks?
> Is she not proud? Doth she not count her blest,
> Unworthy as she is, that we have wrought
> So worthy a gentleman to be her bride?
>
> III.v.142ff

Juliet responds to him:

> Not proud you have, but thankful that you have.
> Proud can I never be of what I hate,
> But thankful even for hate that is meant love.
>
> III.v.147ff

The way she frames her refusal with a rhetoric bespeaking both independence of desire and of judgment, rather than, for example, soliciting her father's understanding or even his mercy, which she might do, without having to reveal her secret, seems to inflame him more than her simple opposition would:

> How, how, how, how, chopped logic! What is this?
> "Proud," and "I thank you," and "I thank you not,"
> And yet "not proud," mistress minion you,
> Thank me no thankings, nor proud me no prouds,
> But fettle your fine joints 'gainst Thursday next,
> To go with Paris to Saint Peter's Church,
> Or I will drag thee on a hurdle thither.
>
> III.v.150ff

Capulet's passion raised, even Juliet's attempt to soften her speech,

> Good father, I beseech you on my knees,
> Hear me with patience but to speak a word[,]
>
> III.v.159f

is useless, for he is consumed by his own fire:

> Hang thee, young baggage! Disobedient wretch!
> I tell thee what: get thee to church a' Thursday,
> Or never after look me in the face.
> Speak not, reply not, do not answer me!
> My fingers itch ....
> .... I do not use to jest.
> Thursday is near, lay hand on heart, advise.
> And you be mine, I'll give you to my friend;
> And you be not, hang, beg, starve, die in the streets[.]
>
> III.v.161ff

This blind, violent, and quick temper in him ought to come as no surprise to a reader or spectator of the play. We have seen Capulet's temper flare at act 1, scene 5, line 76, also in a context yoked to Juliet and Romeo's forbidden love, although at both times he is unaware of the connection.

It is at his ball after his nephew, the equally hot tempered and quick to wrath Tybalt, recognizes, by his voice, that one of the maskers is Romeo. Quick to anger and loyal to the feud between the Montagues and the Capulets, whose passionate hatred breaks out sporadically into civic violence, seething, Tybalt informs Capulet,

> Uncle, there is a Montague, our foe;
> A villain that is hither come in spite
> To scorn at our solemnity this night.
>   I.v.63ff

Capulet notes that it is "young Romeo," and says

> 'A bears him like a portly gentleman;
> And to say truth, Verona brags of him
> To be a virtuous and well-governed youth.
>   I.v.68ff

But this temperate response is not to Tybalt's liking. He responds, "I'll not endure him," and Capulet, patient at first, fumes,

>   He shall be endured.
> What, goodman boy? I say he shall, go to!
> Am I the master here, or you? go to!
> You'll not endure him! God shall mend my soul
> .... go to, go to,
> You are a saucy boy, Is't so indeed?
> This trick may chance to scath you. I know what
> You must contrary me!
>   I.v.78ff

Here as in the scene with Juliet, Capulet shows that he will brook no challenge to his will. He is ruled by the passion of a violent willfulness. Fundamentally implicit in willfulness is the uncompromising need of the will, of the "I want" to assert itself. This need for self-assertion is characteristic not only of the choleric passion shown by Capulet and Tybalt but of Romeo and Juliet's love, also. Characteristic, too, of willfulness is its recklessness, its careening speed. Later, when Romeo demands that Laurence immediately marry him and Juliet, "O, let us hence; I stand on sudden haste," Friar Laurence warns him (without effect) not to be hasty in the execution of his love, cautioning, "Wisely and slow; they stumble that run fast." In the present instance, at Capulet's ball, the nature of the verse Capulet speaks reflects the psychology of willfulness: The rhyme in his couplet,

> What, goodman boy? I say he shall, go to!
> Am I the master here, or you? go to!

cannot wait for completion and discharges itself at the end of the fourth foot of the second line ("or you?") with its reiteration in the fifth ("go to!") suggesting the uncontrollable haste and repetitiveness of anger. *Romeo and Juliet*, then, ostensibly a story of young love and the obstacles which thwart and frustrate it is something more than that. It is an exploration of the willfulness of passion and the passionate nature of willfulness. It provides an anatomy of unreflecting self-assertion, and offers a sermon, one might say, on the consequences wrought when the power of human governance rests with the will, whether will is in the service of amorous or choleric passion.

Shakespeare introduces the theme of "will" explicitly into *Romeo and Juliet* in act 2, scene 3, when Friar Laurence first appears. It is early morning and he is roaming the meadows "culling simples," collecting samples of herbs and flowers which he distills into various medicines and potions, like the one which he later gives to Juliet, which simulates death. As he goes about his labor filling up his "osier cage/ With baleful weeds and precious-juiced flowers," he generalizes about the virtues of the plants he is gathering. He begins with a paradox:

The earth that's nature's mother is her tomb;
What is her burying grave that is her womb,

                                    II.iii.9f

and continues, observing that

... from her womb children of divers kind
We sucking on her natural bosom find,
Many for many virtues excellent,
None but for some and yet all different.
O, mickle is the powerful grace that lies
In herbs, plants, stones, and their true qualities:
For nought so vile that on the earth doth live
But to the earth some special good doth give.

                                    II.iii.11ff

This seems to be an optimistic view of things: there is nothing, no matter how foul seeming, that does not have a virtue and cannot be used well. The virtue of a plant, Laurence observes, is contingent on how it is used, that is on the human understanding of nature. Therefore, the opposing proposition is also true. A plant of good properties can be ill used:

Nor aught so good but strain'd from that fair use
Revolts from true birth, stumbling on abuse:
Virtue itself turns vice, being misapplied[.]

                                    II.iii.19ff

And Laurence gives a specific example from botany to illustrate his law of contraries and usage:

Within the infant rind of this small flower
Poison hath residence and medicine power:
For this, being smelt, with that part cheers each part;
Being tasted, slays all senses with the heart.

                                    II.iii.23ff

Friar Laurence then proceeds to moralize his natural science with an application to human psychology and behavior:

Two such opposed kings encamp them still
In man as well as herbs, grace and rude will;
And where the worser is predominant,
Full soon the canker death eats up that plant.

II.iii.27ff

The exercise of will, Laurence is saying, is like the working of poison. When it governs, death is the result. It is in the realm of one of these kings, Rude Will, that the action of *Romeo and Juliet* takes place. The play demonstrates how the working of Will subverts and prevents the operation of Grace, the unwarranted and unearned, nevertheless manifest gift of heaven's goodness on earth. (For the triumph of grace over will we must wait for Shakespeare's last plays, especially *The Winter's Tale*.)

II. Between Speech and Deed

The context of *Romeo and Juliet* and the importance of that context are established by the sonnet which stands as the play's prologue:

Two households, both alike in dignity,
In fair Verona, where we lay our scene,
From ancient grudge break to new mutiny,
Where civil blood makes civil hands unclean.

Prologue, 1ff

Enmity, violence, and disorder are at the heart of the play, and they spring from a grudge. It is an ancient grudge, of whose effects, but not of whose causes, *Romeo and Juliet* is the anatomy. In the play, the grudge itself stands undefined and, for the meaning and drama of the play, uninteresting and unimportant. The only thing we know and need to know about the actual grudge is its generic nature. A grudge is the resentful response to a perceived slight or insult to one's pride or self-interest. The effects of the grudge, on the other hand, are presented in *Romeo and Juliet* with detailed specificity and a Shakespearean realism which, characteristically, discovers and defines the deepest realities of human experience. Moreover, it is the grudge that gives the love between Romeo and Juliet, the radiant kernel of the play, its richness and its resonance. It is within the context of hate-filled enmity, love's contrast, that the love between Romeo and Juliet achieves its intensity. Romantic love, as opposed to domestic or married love, is a rebellion against the social order and its established values, just as it is a rebellion against time and nature, against aging and alteration. (That's why, according to Friar Laurence's puzzling consolation, they are married best who die married young.) In the case of Romeo and Juliet, it is social disorder which stands opposed to their love. Married love is love which can be integrated into a society, affirming and continuing it. Romantic love threatens society by asserting an untamed, non-conformist, individual will expressed in passionate desire. Romantic love cannot be integrated into society. Such love must itself be vanquished by the opposition it faces and the lovers must be parted, or it must be tamed into domesticity. If neither of these things happens, if the consecration of the love can be neither the separation of the lovers nor marriage, then it must be death, for it is only the immobility of death that can cheat either society or time and nature.

The sonnet's second quatrain summarizes the plot, emphasizing the reciprocal relationship between love and the grudge:

> From forth the fatal loins of these two foes
> A pair of star-cross'd lovers take their life;
> Whose misadventured piteous overthrows
> Do with their death bury their parents' strife.
>
> Prologue, 5f

With a trick of language, Shakespeare introduces the ambiguity which will serve as an engine of the play and a vehicle for the irony which subverts the process of blossoming and turns it into one of withering. The phrase "lovers take their life" signifies both the processes of birth and of death, presaging Friar Laurence's observation that the earth which is nature's mother is also her tomb. That the "suspense" of the plot is undercut by these four lines suggests that we ought to be looking for something else. This suspicion is confirmed by the final quatrain:

> The fearful passage of their death-mark'd love,
> And the continuance of their parents' rage,
> Which, but their children's end, nought could remove,
> Is now the two hours' traffic of our stage[.]
>
> Prologue, 9ff

By giving away the plot and the ending before the play even begins, Shakespeare is directing our attention elsewhere, not to the unfolding of events but to the psychology of actions, so that we may analyze how it is that such a story can happen, how such events may come to be. Thus in *Romeo and Juliet* Shakespeare moves away from the narrative confines of his sources to a psychological analysis of character and event, probing the source of action.

Shakespeare hurls us into the world of enmity, violence, pride, and vanity in the first scene, as he presents the anatomy of a brawl and explores the psychology of men who are blowing themselves up into a passion. It is a scene where none of the capacity for ambiguity and mental flexibility required for understanding the opening sonnet, and the multi-referentiality it prefigures, can exist. The language of the play now involves quibbles, feint-like puns and posturing, not ambiguity. The characters seem essentially empty and bored were it not for the passion and the poses that their participation in the grudge allows them to counterfeit:

> **Sampson**: I strike quickly, being moved.
> **Gregory**: But thou art not quickly moved to strike.
> **Sampson**: A dog of the house of Montague moves me.
> **Gregory**: To move is to stir; and to be valiant is to stand: therefore, if thou art moved, thou runn'st away.
> **Sampson**: A dog of that house shall move me to stand.
>
> I.i.6ff

The scene begins on the streets of Verona where Sampson and Gregory, two of Capulet's servants, are spoiling for a fight, talking tough, bragging sadistically about their sexual prowess and egging each other on until they encounter two of Montague's servants. Pretty quickly the four have exactly what they wanted, something to do which gives them meaning and identity. They exchange taunts and challenges, their swords come out and they are at each other. The reason for the brawl exists only in the determination of the brawlers to brawl. The brawl, of course, attracts more brawlers, partisans of both houses, and men of higher rank than servants, among them Tybalt, Capulet's nephew. He enters the scene just after Benvolio, of the house of Montague, who has drawn his sword to part the brawlers. In the encounter between the two, Shakespeare shows the force of willfulness and the power passion has over reason. The scene also introduces the kind of dramatic confusion which is another one of the engines of the plot in *Romeo and Juliet*. Characters like Tybalt, Mercutio, Capulet, and Romeo and Juliet themselves stubbornly adhere to an overriding passion in order to protect or to justify their positions, their loyalties, their self-conceptions, or their prejudices. The result is a deadly event and a catastrophic consequence:

Benvolio: Part, fools!
Put up your swords; you know not what you do.
Beats down their swords
Enter Tybalt
Tybalt: What, art thou drawn among these heartless hinds?
Turn thee, Benvolio, look upon thy death.
Benvolio: I do but keep the peace: put up thy sword,
Or manage it to part these men with me.
Tybalt: What, drawn, and talk of peace! I hate the word,
As I hate hell, all Montagues, and thee:
Have at thee, coward!

I.i.66ff

They fight, and are joined by others in the brawl, until the two household heads, Capulet and Montague themselves enter the fray, followed by their wives. Their appearance shows not only the extent and depth of their enmity, but its folly and absurdity. They are each aged men whose battling days ought to be behind them, just as, Capulet later laments to a cousin at his ball, their dancing days are (I.v.33). As Capulet rushes in calling for his sword, his wife restrains him with a reproachful mock, "A crutch, a crutch! why call you for a sword?" (I.i.79) Old Montague's wife is even more adamant as her husband rushes to the fray, physically holding him back, insisting, "Thou shalt not stir a foot to seek a foe," as he cries, "Hold me not, let me go." (I.i.82f)

After the Prince and his municipal guard have restrained the brawlers and restored order, Montague, his wife, and Benvolio are left by themselves on the stage. As Old Montague questions Benvolio about how the brawl started, Lady Montague interrupts them, changing the focus of the play from the "pernicious rage" of the grudge to her son, Romeo, as she worries about the melancholy gloom which has been afflicting him and causing him to keep himself removed from social intercourse. He wanders about Verona's woods sleepless before dawn, and when the morning comes, returns to his darkened room to sleep. At his parents' request, Benvolio promises to find out from Romeo the cause of his melancholy. Old Montague and his wife then withdraw when they see Romeo approaching, and Benvolio greets him.

Benvolio: ... What sadness lengthens Romeo's hours?
Romeo: Not having that, which, having, makes them short.
Benvolio: In love?
Romeo: Out—
Benvolio: Of love?
Romeo: Out of her favour, where I am in love.
Benvolio: Alas, that love, so gentle in his view,
Should be so tyrannous and rough in proof!
Romeo: Alas, that love, whose view is muffled still,
Should, without eyes, see pathways to his will!
Where shall we dine?

I.i.166ff

The exchange establishes what might be expected. Romeo is in love, stubbornly and willfully in love, and because his love is unrequited, he is tormented both by desire and by the desire to be in love. Yet there are several disconcerting elements. Perhaps not the least is the way Romeo changes key as he asks, "Where shall we dine?" He is apparently forlorn and melancholy, but suffering no loss of appetite. Perhaps his melancholy is less a result of unrequited love than of his will being slighted and the desire to desire thwarted. When he complains of his beloved Rosaline's failure to reciprocate his love, his complaint sounds less like a desolate lover's anguish than like the response of petulant will to denial or of a man whose self-determining strategies fail, robbing him of the gratification of victory and pride wrought by the successful construction of a successful identity:

> ... she'll not be hit
> With Cupid's arrow; she hath Dian's wit;
> And, in strong proof of chastity well arm'd,
> From love's weak childish bow she lives unharm'd.
> She will not stay the siege of loving terms,
> Nor bide the encounter of assailing eyes,
> Nor ope her lap to saint-seducing gold[.]
>
> I.i.211ff

She's frustrating him, he's complaining. His strategies and his language seem to exist in order to create for himself the identity of a lover rather than either to know, to win, to celebrate or even to lament the loss of his beloved. In one of his lectures on *Romeo and Juliet*, Coleridge says of this love that "Rosaline ... had been a mere name for the yearning of [Romeo's] youthful imagination," that his love for "Rosaline was a mere creation of his fancy; and we should," Coleridge concludes, challenging the authenticity of this love, "remark the boastful positiveness of Romeo in a love of his own making, which is never shown where love is really near the heart."[2] That Romeo's love is motivated in great measure by the will to be in love and to fashion for himself, thereby, an identity ought not to be seen as particularly strange from a historical or a cultural point of view as well as from the psychological one which Coleridge offers. Romeo is following in a tradition of love and the willful creation of identity that had been developing throughout the Renaissance in such consciousness-shaping writers as Petrarch, Andreas Capelanus, and Baldassare Castiglione. Benjamin Boysen, discussing Petrarch's view of love, explains that "[i]n his *Rerum vulgarium fragmenta*, Petrarch demonstrates" that

> [l]ove is at one and the same time that which creates his identity, and that which dissolves it anew, it is simultaneously creation and destruction, recognition and alienation, pleasure and suffering—life and death.... The project of the poet is monological, and he strives toward a unity with himself, actualized in a circular and narcissistic auto-communication in which he ... listens to his own speech.... He has to express himself in the other in order to appear to himself.... He [the poet as conceived by Petrarch] has a strong inclination toward being solitary, unique, independent, and self-enclosed.... However, he [Petrarch] often emphasizes that self-consciousness must make the detour by the other, if it is to achieve understanding and consciousness of itself. (*Orbis Litterarum* Vol 58, No 3 [June 2003], 163)

The beloved serves to define the lover to himself.

In *The Art of Courtly Love* (c. 1147), Andreas Capelanus set down the conventions of courtly love, particularly valorizing the condition of being in love. He established the nobility of the lover's worshipful attitude towards his beloved and outlined the rituals of a lover's devotion. Castiglione's *The Courtier* (published in 1528), is a sort of handbook defining how character ought to be formed, what attitudes ought to be developed, which accomplishments are worthy, and how one ought to behave. It was written in the form of a conversation between a group of men and women in which they try to discover what elements are essential to the formation of an ideal identity. Romeo's chief failing as a lover and as a poet when we first see him is his lack of what Castiglione calls *sprezzatura*, the primary requisite of an accomplished person: the effortlessness which must characterize everything one does.

Romeo's failure in love, thus, is a failure in self-creation and a frustration of his will. His love of Rosaline shows the strain of an adolescent attempt at the creation of an identity. This failure is particularly apparent in the conventionality of his poetry when we first see him. Love is for the lover an occasion for self-invention through poetry, for the sensuous, inventive linguistic expression of an internal, invisible experience. Romeo's lovelorn state provides him an identity to conceptualize through his speech and his condition becomes the subject of his poetry, and because it is different from what he wishes it to be it is full of paradox and oxymoron, just as, according to Petrarch, is the nature of love itself as it affects the lover. Romeo's effort is to create an image of himself as lithe and supple in perception and understanding, but the self he is figuring is a defeated self, absorbed in its own defeat. Its object, the unresponsive beloved, does not cooperate in his project of self-construction. Construction of a self whose very sense of selfhood is being thwarted is a difficult task for poetry, and Romeo's poetry, too, at this point in the play is a failed poetry. While the sincerity of Romeo's love and of his verse, then, may be open to doubt, the sincerity of his pose can not be. He plays the lover searching in himself for a poetics of love to express himself, and he comes up with the conventional melancholy stuff of a rejected lover, reflecting the insincerity of his love rather than the anguish of grief:

> Love is a smoke raised with the fume of sighs;
> Being purged, a fire sparkling in lovers' eyes;
> Being vex'd a sea nourish'd with lovers' tears:
> What is it else? a madness most discreet,
> A choking gall and a preserving sweet.
>
> I.i.193ff

This is the sort of thing Shakespeare has had fun with when he's given verse like it to the rustic characters in *As You Like It*. It is also the kind of exercise he will assign to Troilus in *Troilus and Cressida*, who is in love with an image of himself which blinds him to the realities around him whether regarding matters of love or war. We must remember it later on when Romeo meets Juliet and finds authentic and unstrained poetry, needing no bridges like "What is it else?"

The dangerous capacity of language to create or induce belief in a false or self-constructed reality plays a pivotal role in the famous balcony scene between the lovers, too, when even at the intense height of passionate sincerity, Juliet nearly reproaches Romeo for attempting poetry when he endeavors to convey the strength of his constancy:

Juliet: ....
Dost thou love me? I know thou wilt say 'Ay,'
And I will take thy word: yet if thou swear'st,
Thou mayst prove false; at lovers' perjuries
They say, Jove laughs. O gentle Romeo,
If thou dost love, pronounce it faithfully:
Romeo: Lady, by yonder blessed moon I swear
That tips with silver all these fruit-tree tops—
Juliet: O, swear not by the moon, the inconstant moon,
That monthly changes in her circled orb,
Lest that thy love prove likewise variable.
Romeo: What shall I swear by?
Juliet: Do not swear at all;
Or, if thou wilt, swear by thy gracious self,
Which is the god of my idolatry,
And I'll believe thee.
Romeo: If my heart's dear love—
Juliet: Well, do not swear: although I joy in thee,
I have no joy of this contract to-night:
It is too rash, too unadvised, too sudden;
Too like the lightning, which doth cease to be
Ere one can say 'It lightens.'

II.ii.90ff

35

The transition from talking about himself and his love to talking about the feud between Montagues and Capulets is effortless when Romeo notices the remnants of the brawl as he and Benvolio amble about. The language he uses to consider the enmity, for example, is in the same style as the language he has just used when speaking about himself. His speech essentially is formed of yoked opposites like "brawling love," "loving hate," "heavy lightness," "serious vanity," "mis-shapen chaos of well-seeming forms," "feather of lead," "bright smoke," "cold fire," "sick health," or "still-waking sleep," willful constructions, oxymora which play with paradox and postulate the identity of opposites. The brawl, too, is an opportunity for self-construction, but as a poet, rather than as a partisan combatant. Romeo's initial observation regarding the recent melee: "Here's much to do with hate, but more with love," is particularly significant just because it is puzzling. Certainly, there is much to do with hate. Hate, however, as interpreted by Romeo's paradox is the outgrowth of self-love. One needs a hated other to assert his own full identity, just as Romeo needs a beloved to know his, and the love of Juliet and Romeo needs opposition to achieve its full tragic intensity. There is, in the execution of any grudge, much to do with self-love and with nursing injuries or slights to one's sense of self and of self-esteem. There is in the holding of a grudge a willful assertion of *amour propre*. Like passionate, sexual, romantic love, hate is fueled by a passion full of self and the one who hates depends upon his adversary for his identity as surely as the lover needs the beloved for his own authenticity.

III. Words as Things

The willful construction of identity through language and the use of language as an indication of will are repeatedly developed in *Romeo and Juliet*, not just in the character of Romeo. The brawling servants of the first scene have no other identities but the ones they express in their allegiances regarding the conflict between the two houses. Capulet's identifying characteristics are his indomitable will and the choleric expression of it. Tybalt is entirely defined by "willful choler." It is, however, undoubtedly in the character of Mercutio that Shakespeare most clearly presents both the construction of identity through the construction of a purely linguistic persona and the assertion of a willful identity through language. Dramatically, Mercutio serves as a simple, although decisive, plot device: in act 3, scene 1, his goading engages Tybalt in combat after Romeo has declined to react to Tybalt's provocations, and it is Mercutio's death in that duel with Tybalt, caused more by Romeo's intervention—in an attempt to stop the fight—than by Tybalt's skill, that leads Romeo to kill Tybalt in self-reproachful and vengeful fury. But Mercutio's role and, consequently, his function in the play are far greater than his overt action or his function as a device to propel the plot. He not only embodies the role of language in the creation of character; the character, Mercutio, is used to provide a linguistic context which serves the construction of psychological texture and depth.

Mercutio, for example, sets the tone of sexual intensity which is implicit in and suggested by the balcony scene in which Romeo and Juliet declare their love. The balcony scene follows quickly after the scene at Capulet's ball, where the lovers first meet. But standing between that scene and the balcony scene are a choral sonnet which introduces the new love and the hindrances it must overcome and a scene in which Mercutio and Benvolio search for Romeo, who has gone off on his own at the end of Capulet's ball. Mercutio surmises that Romeo has gone home to bed, but Benvolio says he thinks he saw Romeo scale Capulet's garden wall (which, in fact, is the case), and tells Mercutio, "Call, good Mercutio." Mercutio responds, "Nay, I'll conjure too," mocking at the same time Romeo's pose as a (conventional) lover and poet:

Romeo! humours! madman! passion! lover!
Appear thou in the likeness of a sigh:
Speak but one rhyme, and I am satisfied;
Cry but 'Ay me!' pronounce but 'love' and 'dove[.]'
II.i.7ff

But Romeo does not appear and Mercutio, characteristically, continues, enticing him with Rosaline's features:

The ape is dead, and I must conjure him.
I conjure thee by Rosaline's bright eyes,
By her high forehead and her scarlet lip,
By her fine foot, straight leg and quivering thigh [,]
                                                II.i.16ff

and then mocks these conventional and rarifying phrases with a bawdy turn:

And the demesnes that there adjacent lie.

Benvolio stops him, warning, "if he hear thee, thou wilt anger him," but Mercutio, rather than being halted, uses this admonition as a spur to drive through even riskier linguistic terrain, mined with double entendres.

This cannot anger him: 'twould anger him
To raise a spirit in his mistress' circle
Of some strange nature, letting it there stand
Till she had laid it and conjured it down;
That were some spite: my invocation
Is fair and honest, and in his mistress' name
I conjure only but to raise up him.
                                                II.i.23ff

Thus Mercutio leaves in the reader's or the spectator's mind a sense both of the sexual intensity which is a part of Romeo and Juliet's love and the suggestion of a solely sexual passion, which misses entirely the qualities of sanctity, seriousness, and devotion which characterize their love.

Mercutio's most famous speech, however, the Queen Mab speech, a great set piece in a play with many memorable set pieces, seems to have absolutely nothing to do with the action of the play. In that respect it is unlike his conjuring speech which provides the ground bass against which the melodies and harmonies of the balcony scene play out and also unlike the linguistically gorgeous balcony scene itself. Although the balcony scene is a poetic *tour de force*, it also constitutes the essential action of the play. Without the poetry of the balcony scene, we should have to take the love between Romeo and Juliet—and its sacredness—on faith, something asserted rather than demonstrated. But by the quality of its poetry, the balcony scene represents materially and sensuously the strength of their love, the force which must overwhelm and propel them, the passion to which they become enslaved.

Mercutio's Queen Mab speech is a mythopoeic interpretation of dreams. He improvises it on the way to Capulet's party to show off his wit. It is woven into the play the way a song is often fitted into a musical. Romeo comments that he has had disturbing dreams, which leads to a witty duel of words between him and Mercutio

> **Romeo**: ... we mean well in going to this mask;
> But 'tis no wit to go.
> **Mercutio**: Why, may one ask?
> **Romeo**: I dream'd a dream to-night.
> **Mercutio**: And so did I.
> **Romeo**: Well, what was yours?
> **Mercutio**: That dreamers often lie.
> **Romeo**: In bed asleep, while they do dream things true.
>
> I.iv.47ff

This dueling recitative in which words change their meanings in a flash culminates in Mercutio's "aria" which begins, "O, then, I see Queen Mab hath been with you." And his invention is off at full speed for more than forty lines, perhaps producing in the reader or the spectator something of the impatience that helps precipitate the lovers' death. What Mercutio is doing in this speech, however, is turning words into visual imagery in order to convey the working of an invisible force which has the power to create the experience of phantom images. It is just what Shakespeare is doing in this play, which is, after all, showing visible representation of such invisible, intangible, but real forces as love and resentment:

> She is the fairies' midwife, and she comes
> In shape no bigger than an agate-stone
> On the fore-finger of an alderman,
> Drawn with a team of little atomies
> Athwart men's noses as they lie asleep;
> Her wagon-spokes made of long spiders' legs,
> The cover of the wings of grasshoppers,
> The traces of the smallest spider's web,
> The collars of the moonshine's watery beams,
> Her whip of cricket's bone, the lash of film,
> Her wagoner a small grey-coated gnat,
> Not so big as a round little worm
> ....
> Her chariot is an empty hazel-nut.
>
> I.iv.54ff

In the Queen Mab speech, Mercutio is representing the spurs of desire by the miniature world of the fairies, the forces which he fancies that activate human desires as they are experienced in dreams through the imaginary stimulation of the various sensory organs:

> .... she gallops night by night
> Through lovers' brains, and then they dream of love;
> O'er courtiers' knees, that dream on court'sies straight,
> O'er lawyers' fingers, who straight dream on fees,
> O'er ladies' lips, who straight on kisses dream,
> ....
> Sometime she gallops o'er a courtier's nose,
> And then dreams he of smelling out a suit;
> And sometime comes she with a tithe-pig's tail
> Tickling a parson's nose as a' lies asleep,
> Then dreams, he of another benefice:
> Sometime she driveth o'er a soldier's neck,
> And then dreams he of cutting foreign throats.
>
> I.iv.70ff

As he continues in his speech, however, Mercutio shows Mab as a harbinger of ill-fortune as well as a stimulator of desire, showing a deeper mischief in her:

> .... This is that very Mab
> That plats the manes of horses in the night,
> And bakes the elflocks in foul sluttish hairs,
> Which once untangled, much misfortune bodes.
>
> I.iv.88ff

The motif that Friar Laurence will later develop of contradictory capabilities cohabiting within a single substance, of the co-presence of birth and death, or of healing and wounding, which we have already encountered in the opening sonnet, is sounded here. Finally, Romeo stops him crying, "Peace, peace, Mercutio, peace! Thou talk'st of nothing." He admits it readily. "True, I talk of dreams," he says, unthwarted by the interruption, and continues with a riff on a new theme—

> Which are the children of an idle brain,
> Begot of nothing but vain fantasy,
> Which is as thin of substance as the air
> And more inconstant than the wind, who wooes
> Even now the frozen bosom of the north,
> And, being anger'd, puffs away from thence,
> Turning his face to the dew-dropping south.

—until this time Benvolio stops him with a segue, saying,

> This wind, you talk of, blows us from ourselves;
> Supper is done, and we shall come too late.
>
> I.iv.97ff

But with this innocent riposte by which Benvolio is simply trying to match Mercutio's wit, Shakespeare makes the language of the play the harbinger of future tragedy, a premonitory allusion to the time when Juliet will wake too late in the tomb to meet not Romeo but death.

IV. Words as Determinants

When Lady Capulet broaches the subject of marriage with Juliet in act 1, scene 3, she begins with the general question, "How stands your disposition to be married?" It is less a question, however, than an announcement of what is on the agenda for Juliet and that Juliet will be required to conform to it. Juliet answers skillfully: "It is an honor that I dream not of." Juliet's nurse is impressed with the answer:

> An honour! were not I thine only nurse,
> I would say thou hadst suck'd wisdom from thy teat.
>
> I.iii.67f

Why should this reply create such a response in the nurse? It is true that the nurse is a figure defined by her vain and comic garrulity, just as Mercutio is defined by his romantic eloquence. Juliet's nurse's long and colorful digression in this scene, however, in which she remembers a fall Juliet took as a child and her husband's bawdy response as well as Juliet's precocious answer—

> .... she broke her brow:
> And then my husband—God be with his soul!
> A' was a merry man—took up the child:
> 'Yea,' quoth he, 'dost thou fall upon thy face?
> Thou wilt fall backward when thou hast more wit;
> Wilt thou not, Jule?' and, by my holidame,
> The pretty wretch left crying and said 'Ay.'
> ....I never should forget it:
> 'Wilt thou not, Jule?' quoth he;
> And, pretty fool, it stinted and said 'Ay.'
>
> I.iii.38ff

is not merely a comic routine, nor only a painfully comic forecast of the impending tragedy, but an important portrayal of the nurse's character. It is the nurse who will serve as the go-between for Romeo and Juliet before they are married and she will provide them with the conventional machinery of forbidden romance—a rope ladder for Romeo to climb up to Juliet's window, for example—on their marriage night. She is, as her ribald speech suggests, "partly a bawd," and her abandonment of Juliet, when she advises in act 4 that Juliet forget her marriage vows to Romeo and marry Paris, show in her a bawd's honor.

In the present circumstance, regarding Juliet's answer to her mother, it is fair to say that the nurse is not being garrulous but recognizes Juliet's gentle diplomacy and charming equivocation—the tactics she will attempt to use so unsuccessfully later with her father—in the face of her mother's subtle but firm manipulation. Juliet's mother is less sympathetic to her daughter's character than the nurse and sticks to the issue:

> Well, think of marriage now; younger than you,
> Here in Verona, ladies of esteem,
> Are made already mothers: by my count,
> I was your mother much upon these years
> That you are now a maid. Thus then in brief:
> The valiant Paris seeks you for his love.
> ....
> What say you? Can you love the gentleman?
> ....
> Speak briefly, can you like of Paris' love?
> I.iii.69ff

Characteristically, and evasively, Juliet answers:

> I'll look to like, if looking liking move:
> But no more deep will I endart mine eye
> Than your consent gives strength to make it fly.
> I.iii.97ff

This is exactly the tone and the sort of rhetoric that will later so infuriate her father. In this instance, however, she is not told to look me no looking and like me no liking. Her mother does not reproach her subtle and playful mind. She ignores it.

This is the way Juliet speaks, and Juliet is not offering opposition to parental authority. She is, in fact, respecting it. "No more deep will [she] endart her eye/ Than [her parents'] consent gives strength to make it fly." As they set out for the festivities, Lady Capulet reminds Juliet that "the County stays," Paris is waiting for her to make her appearance and to make up her mind, too. This last reminder and the tenor of her preceding remarks lend to Lady Capulet's speech a hint of pandering:

> Read o'er the volume of young Paris' face,
> And find delight writ there with beauty's pen;
> Examine every married lineament,
> And see how one another lends content
> And what obscured in this fair volume lies
> Find written in the margent of his eyes.
>   I.iii.81ff

Although talking specifically about Paris, Lady Capulet has told Juliet that she is now sexually ripe, that she ought to look at men and she is also telling her what to look for in men and how to look for it. She is also letting Juliet know that her newly defined power of desire and her newly defined state of being desirable are not to be under her own governance but her parents'. We have heard enough of Juliet already to mark by her language that she is a daughter with a will of her own and a disposition to find and direct her own course. As a rule, daughters in Shakespeare's plays are independent in nature and tend to be inclined to follow their own prompting, even when it means defiance of their fathers' will. Without intending to, Lady Capulet is preparing Juliet for her meeting with Romeo at the ball.

The encounter between Romeo and Juliet is, foremost, a discovery of a mutual language, and they create the bond of their love by the complicity of their language. Their meeting is a scene of rare delicacy, embedded in the violence which surrounds and will destroy them. We are reminded of their doom by the immediate proximity of Tybalt and his malicious vow of retribution for his uncle's wrath when he expresses his anger at Romeo's presence at Capulet's dance:

> Patience perforce with willful choler meeting
> Makes my flesh tremble in their different greeting.
> I will withdraw: but this intrusion shall
> Now seeming sweet convert to bitter gall.
>
> I.v.91ff

When he arrives at Capulet's ball Romeo is a failed lover, more in love with the melancholy image of himself that failure has engendered than with his presumed beloved, Rosaline. On the way to the ball, as we have seen in discussing Mercutio's Queen Mab speech, Romeo has been bantering with Mercutio, but then he changes the tone of his speech and expresses a foreboding which he cannot explain. The ground is not firm under his feet, but he willfully abandons himself to a devil-may-care recklessness:

> ... my mind misgives
> Some consequence yet hanging in the stars
> Shall bitterly begin his fearful date
> With this night's revels and expire the term
> Of a despised life closed in my breast
> By some vile forfeit of untimely death.
> But He, that hath the steerage of my course,
> Direct my sail! On, lusty gentlemen.
>
> I.iv.106ff

This is a pessimistic, almost spiteful surrender to fate, spiteful because he does not believe in the beneficence of providence as, for example, Posthumus Leonatus does in *Cymbeline*, one of Shakespeare's last plays, at V.iii. 41–46, when he utters similar words but frames them in a major key, "The heavens still must work.... Fortune brings in some boats that are not steer'd."

Shakespeare achieves the sense of the immediate, unifying, passionate, intimate, and playful complicity which characterizes the love between Romeo and Juliet by presenting their first conversation in the form of a sonnet which they spontaneously compose together:

> **Romeo**: If I profane with my unworthiest hand
> This holy shrine, the gentle fine is this:
> My lips, two blushing pilgrims, ready stand
> To smooth that rough touch with a tender kiss.
> Juliet: Good pilgrim, you do wrong your hand too much,
> Which mannerly devotion shows in this;
> For saints have hands that pilgrims' hands do touch,
> And palm to palm is holy palmers' kiss.
> **Romeo**: Have not saints lips, and holy palmers too?
> **Juliet**: Ay, pilgrim, lips that they must use in prayer.
> **Romeo**: O, then, dear saint, let lips do what hands do;
> They pray, grant thou, lest faith turn to despair.
> **Juliet**: Saints do not move, though grant for prayers' sake.
> **Romeo**: Then move not, while my prayer's effect I take.
>
> I.v.95ff

As the lips join the lovers together in a kiss and make them one, more than just symbolically, so the sonnet joins them together making their separate utterance one unified poetic form.

But even as they are becoming one, the forces that will tear them asunder are working around them, framing their love. Just as their sonnet follows directly, as we have seen, on Tybalt's curse, so their dialogue, following that sonnet, is interrupted by Juliet's mother. As Romeo speaks of the kiss they have just exchanged—"Thus from my lips, by yours, my sin is purged," and Juliet responds, "Then have my lips the sin that they have took," which Romeo converts into an opportunity for a second kiss, "Sin from thy lips? O trespass sweetly urged! Give me my sin again," and Juliet teases him, saying, "You kiss by the book,"—Juliet's nurse steps in, telling Juliet, "Madam, your mother craves a word with you."

There are hardly any stage directions in Shakespearean texts, and when there are they are scant, usually only indicating exits and entrances. Consequently, the business around the words on the page, the action one might expect to see on the stage, must be imagined by the reader relying on the text itself, just as it must be derived and blocked from the dialogue by a director for a stage production. In this instance, if there were a stage direction in the text, it very likely would read something like,

(*Lady Capulet, seeing Juliet flirting with a young man who is not Paris, sends the nurse over to break it up.*) **Nurse:** Madam, your mother craves a word with you.

Off Juliet goes, perhaps blushing, perhaps giving Romeo an exasperated smile, or a look of longing and desire, and her mother does some distracting or reprimanding business with her. Romeo then uses this opportunity to ask the nurse, "What [who]is her mother?" and the nurse replies, "Her mother is the lady of the house." "Is she a Capulet?" Romeo says to himself. "O dear account! my life is my foe's debt." A few lines later, as the guests are leaving (and Juliet is no longer having a word with her mother) she asks the nurse to tell her the names of the departing guests. By this ruse she discovers the name of the stranger with whom she exchanged the lines of a sonnet and two kisses.

Go ask his name: if he be married.
My grave is like to be my wedding bed.

Her words sting with irony, for her grave will be her wedding bed precisely because Romeo is not married. The nurse returns and tells her,

His name is Romeo, and a Montague;
The only son of your great enemy.

And Juliet says to herself,

My only love sprung from my only hate!
Too early seen unknown, and known too late!
Prodigious birth of love it is to me,

That I must love a loathed enemy.

I.v.136ff

Embedded in this flowering of love is the problem of what actually constitutes identity, which Juliet proclaims two scenes later from her balcony—

What's in a name? that which we call a rose
By any other name would smell as sweet[,]

II.ii.43f

the thing itself or the words which point to it? Juliet obviously thinks it is the thing itself not the identity attached to it by disfiguring or falsifying words. Yet for most of the characters in the play the words which identify a thing have become its essentials and are thought to be embodied in it.

V. Will, Speech, and Control

When Paris first lets Capulet know he'd like to marry Juliet, Capulet's response is neither intemperate nor autocratic:

My child is yet a stranger in the world;
She hath not seen the change of fourteen years,
Let two more summers wither in their pride,
Ere we may think her ripe to be a bride.

I.ii.8ff

When Paris presses him, saying, "Younger than she are happy mothers made," Capulet responds with the caution he himself later forgets, a caution quite similar to the warning Friar Laurence offers Romeo about the dangers of being hasty, "And too soon marr'd are those so early made." Nevertheless, Capulet encourages Paris to pursue his hope but adds what, once again, he will later forget, that his approval depends on Juliet's acceptance of Paris,

But woo her, gentle Paris, get her heart,

My will to her consent is but a part; An she agree, within her scope of choice
Lies my consent and fair according voice.

I.ii.16ff

When he abandons his position the reasons are as unstated as the reasons for the grudge/ feud between the houses of Capulet and Montague itself. They are never presented and must be inferred—or dismissed as dramatically irrelevant. What moves the action of the play and creates the drama, conflict, and tension is the decision, one may assert, not the reason for the decision. But the richness of Shakespearean drama results from the depth of character construction, from the portrayal of human authenticity. Shakespeare's characters are alive because they can be moved and determined by thought or feeling which may even be hidden from themselves as well as from us. That is why, to use the distinction Erich Auerbach makes in his essay "Odysseus' Scar" in *Mimesis*, the plays can be interpreted as well as analyzed.

In Capulet's case, once asserted, it is clear, his will does not bend. When his pride is at stake he is inflexible. It is essential to him to define himself as being in control, and it is second nature to him not to tolerate a challenge to that power. At the time Paris first informs Capulet of his desire to marry Juliet, when Capulet is temperate, Capulet's aim is to present himself as a judicious and fair father. Perhaps he is reluctant, without even consciously knowing it, to cede to any man the primacy over Juliet he would lose to her husband, and his temperance cloaks his will to retain possession. He can, in any event, be proud to show his benevolence. His power seems not forced and autocratic, but liberal and genial. What then makes Capulet stake his honor on revising that image of himself and presume to say,

.... I will make a desperate tender
Of my child's love: I think she will be ruled
In all respects by me; nay, more, I doubt it not[?]

III.iv.12ff

And why is it "a desperate" offer he makes? He does not explain himself. For the reader or spectator, his words have an eerie and ironic resonance, for unbeknownst to himself, he is speaking a terrible truth. He will make a terrible sacrifice of his daughter's love, turning Juliet into a kind of Iphegenia. Although he does not know it, he is giving up his daughter as a sacrificial offering to allay the gods of the feud. Her death will restore the harmonious winds of social peace to Verona, ending the feud between the two houses. When he says he "thinks she will be ruled/ In all respects by me," he is not really "thinking." He is boasting of his power of possession, asserting his own confidence in himself as if saying, "I have faith in my power over her will," and he caps it with a self-congratulatory, "more, I doubt it not." Later, he asserts his sense of ownership of her quite directly in his fit in act 3, scene 5, line 193 (But Juliet's will is not less stark than his, and their encounter proves explosive.) Why does he call his offer desperate if at he thinks, however, that Juliet will be ruled by him? The risk, in his mind, cannot be with regard to Juliet, an unconscious premonition of her true nature, but to his own power to be in control, simply to be in control, at a moment when that power of his has been threatened. Look at the context of his tender.

> Things have fall'n out, sir, so unluckily,
> That we have had no time to move our daughter:
> Look you, she loved her kinsman Tybalt dearly,
> And so did I:— Well, we were born to die.
>
> III.iv.1ff

His words make it sound like Capulet has accepted the limits of mortality and therefore the limitations of his will: "we were born to die," he says in apparent resignation. But he immediately shows that he has not accepted such limitation. No more than in the scene with Tybalt at the ball or in the scene with Juliet later when he explodes at her refusal to marry Paris has he resigned his will and his need to be in control. Rather, characteristically, when his will is opposed, as we have seen, he defies opposition with a stronger assertion of will.

This is what he does in the scene with Paris when he unconditionally offers him Juliet in marriage bypassing the need to obtain her consent, and yoking her desire to his will. Death has momentarily challenged his sense of the power and the finality of his will, and the desperate tender he makes is a bet against death's power. Capulet sacrifices Juliet to death in a contest with death for the power to be in control of events.

This is clearly evident in act 4, scene 2. Juliet has, for all appearances, capitulated to her father's wishes. She has gone to Friar Laurence's cell, her family thinks, to make confession before her wedding. Really she has gone to plan how she and Romeo will be reunited and to get from Laurence the fatal sleeping potion. Her father, now believing she has abjured her "self-willed harlotry," is in an affectionate and expansive mood. He is reassured in his possession of her, even as he gives her away, for it is according to his will. He greets her teasingly, alluding to her rebelliousness as if it were a cute misdemeanor, saying: "How now, my headstrong! where have you been gadding? She replies with seeming openness but full of guile:

> Where I have learn'd me to repent the sin
> Of disobedient opposition
> To you and your behests, and am enjoin'd
> By holy Laurence to fall prostrate here,
> And beg your pardon: pardon, I beseech you!
> Henceforward I am ever ruled by you.
>
> IV.ii.16ff

It is exactly what he wants to hear, especially her promise to be ruled by him—forever! and despite, as Cordelia, in *King Lear*, reminds *her* father, the fact that she is about to have a husband by whom she is obliged to be ruled!—and he responds: "Why, I am glad on't; this is well: stand up:/ This is as't should be." Notice he does not say, "this is as I want it," but "This is as't should be." He's in control!

Of Capulet, as of Lear, of whom he is a foreshadowing, it can be said, "he hath ever but slenderly known himself." (*King Lear* I.i.294) Just as his motives for casting Juliet without her consent onto Paris are not stated, so, it appears, they are not even known to him. Like his daughter and her beloved, he simply is hurtling headlong willfully in the direction his desire propels him, defiant of the overwhelming limitations of mortality. This is what the Greeks meant by hybris, and in this case, it is what makes the tragedy of Romeo and Juliet as much the tragedy of Juliet's father as of the lovers.

VI. The Failure of Words to Change the Course of Things

Once it is set in motion by the meeting of the lovers, the action of *Romeo and Juliet* is swift, and hurtles to its climax, despite the many decorative rhetorical and comic flourishes which seem to keep the plot from achieving completion. The action pulls against the words. The nurse, for example, acting as go-between strains Juliet's patience by her inability to deliver Romeo's answer quickly regarding when and where they are to meet in order to marry:

> **Nurse**: I am a-weary, give me leave awhile:
> Fie, how my bones ache! what a jaunt have I had!
> **Juliet**: I would thou hadst my bones, and I thy news:
> ....
> **Nurse**: Jesu, what haste? can you not stay awhile?
> Do you not see that I am out of breath?

Juliet shows the same aptness now to distinguish between words and reality in the apparently comic colloquy with the nurse that she showed when she stopped Romeo, below her window in her father's orchard, from swearing by the moon.

> **Juliet**: How art thou out of breath, when thou hast breath
> To say to me that thou art out of breath?

But this does not hasten the nurse, who with words creates Romeo for herself and savors him.

> **Nurse**: Well, you have made a simple choice; you know not
> how to choose a man: Romeo! no, not he; though his

face be better than any man's, yet his leg excels
all men's; and for a hand, and a foot, and a body,
though they be not to be talked on, yet they are
past compare: he is not the flower of courtesy,
but, I'll warrant him, as gentle as a lamb. Go thy
ways, wench; serve God. What, have you dined at home?
Juliet: No, no: but all this did I know before.
What says he of our marriage? what of that?

But the nurse is still not ready, asserting her own need over
Juliet's:

> **Nurse**: Lord, how my head aches! what a head have I!
> It beats as it would fall in twenty pieces.
> My back o' t' other side,—O, my back, my back!
> ....
> **Juliet:** I' faith, I am sorry that thou art not well.
> Sweet, sweet, sweet nurse, tell me, what says my love?
> **Nurse**: Your love says, like an honest gentleman, and a
> courteous, and a kind, and a handsome, and, I
> warrant, a virtuous,—Where is your mother?
> **Juliet**: Where is my mother! why, she is within;
> Where should she be? How oddly thou repliest!
> 'Your love says, like an honest gentleman,
> Where is your mother?'
>
> II.v.25ff

The exchange is comic, and it shows how self-indulgent, even
willful the nurse is and how much it comes out in her love of
hearing herself talk, but it also reproduces the tension of
impatience, of conflict between the will of an impulse and the
resistance it meets. Friar Laurence's speeches also retard the
plot as much as they propel it in the long lectures he delivers
to Romeo. In the following citation he is responding to
Romeo's disconsolate threat to end his own life after he has
been banished from Mantua (and, therefore, Juliet) after
killing Tybalt:

Hold thy desperate hand: ....
....
I thought thy disposition better temper'd.
Hast thou slain Tybalt? wilt thou slay thyself?
And slay thy lady too that lives in thee,
By doing damned hate upon thyself?
Why rail'st thou on thy birth, the heaven, and earth?
Since birth, and heaven, and earth, all three do meet
In thee at once; which thou at once wouldst lose.
Fie, fie, thou shamest thy shape, thy love, thy wit;
Which, like a usurer, abound'st in all,
And usest none in that true use indeed
Which should bedeck thy shape, thy love, thy wit:
Thy noble shape is but a form of wax,
Digressing from the valour of a man;
Thy dear love sworn but hollow perjury,
Killing that love which thou hast vow'd to cherish;
Thy wit, that ornament to shape and love,
Misshapen in the conduct of them both,
Like powder in a skitless soldier's flask,
Is set afire by thine own ignorance,
And thou dismember'd with thine own defence.

Friar Laurence is repeating the theme he introduced in his flower speech: our virtues and our failings depend on how we use our powers. But the lesson is hardly useful to Romeo even when Laurence shows him the bright side of things:

What, rouse thee, man! thy Juliet is alive,
For whose dear sake thou wast but lately dead;
There art thou happy: Tybalt would kill thee,
But thou slew'st Tybalt; there are thou happy too:
The law that threaten'd death becomes thy friend
And turns it to exile; there art thou happy:
A pack of blessings lights up upon thy back;
Happiness courts thee in her best array;
But, like a misbehaved and sullen wench,

Thou pout'st upon thy fortune and thy love:
Take heed, take heed, for such die miserable.

It is only when his words become congruent with Romeo's desire that they become effective. Then Friar Laurence is not a dispassionate preacher whose allegiance is to the soul's correction. Despite his earlier, insightful words about grace and rude will, he is a chief practitioner of willfulness in *Romeo and Juliet* intent on shaping the lovers' story to his will despite its apparently destined course, something he realizes too late when he flees from Juliet's tomb in the last act of the play. Now he spurs Romeo on:

Go, get thee to thy love, as was decreed,
Ascend her chamber, hence and comfort her:
But look thou stay not till the watch be set,
For then thou canst not pass to Mantua;
Where thou shalt live, till we can find a time
To blaze your marriage, reconcile your friends,
Beg pardon of the prince, and call thee back
With twenty hundred thousand times more joy
Than thou went'st forth in lamentation.
Go before, nurse: commend me to thy lady;
And bid her hasten all the house to bed,
Which heavy sorrow makes them apt unto:
Romeo is coming.

III.iii.108ff

For Romeo the lesson is short lived and entirely contingent upon apparent circumstance, as his impatient accession to despair when he hears (falsely) of Juliet's death will show.

The lovers themselves enjoy idyllic moments together in which time is almost suspended even as its onrushing force presses against them. And the chief source of their trouble is that their love and their will are powerless to alter reality. Not by the stubborn insistence of language nor by the sacrificial devotion of love can they stop the movement of the hours or redefine day and night. Only death can still time.

Juliet: Wilt thou be gone? it is not yet near day:
It was the nightingale, and not the lark,
That pierced the fearful hollow of thine ear;
....
Romeo: It was the lark, the herald of the morn,
No nightingale: look, love, what envious streaks
Do lace the severing clouds in yonder east:
Night's candles are burnt out, and jocund day
Stands tiptoe on the misty mountain tops.
....
Juliet: Yon light is not day-light, I know it, I:
It is some meteor that the sun exhales,
To be to thee this night a torch-bearer,
And light thee on thy way to Mantua:
Therefore stay yet; thou need'st not to be gone.
Romeo: Let me be ta'en, let me be put to death;
I am content, so thou wilt have it so.
I'll say yon grey is not the morning's eye,
....
Juliet: It is, it is: hie hence, be gone, away!

III.v.1ff

VII. The Powerlessness of Will

After Friar Laurence gives Juliet the sleeping potion, he writes
to Romeo, banished in Mantua,

> [t]hat he should hither [to Juliet's tomb] come ... this dire
>   night,
> To help to take her from her borrow'd grave,
>
> V.iii.247f

This did not happen because

> ... he which bore my letter, Friar John,
> Was stay'd by accident, and yesternight
> Return'd my letter back.
>
> V.iii.251ff

The messenger whom Laurence sent to tell Romeo of the plan to reunite him and Juliet and spirit them away from Verona under the cover of death and banishment is prevented from delivering his message when he is quarantined in a sick man's house. Thus on the strength of an accident by which human will is thwarted, the climax of the feud, with its propulsive violence is set in motion. Romeo hears only the (false) news that Juliet is actually dead. In despair and in the sort of haste against which Laurence earlier warned, Romeo buys a dram of poison from a poor apothecary in Mantua and arrives at Juliet's tomb moments before she awakes and moments before Laurence arrives to inform her that Romeo has not gotten his message, of which mischance he himself has just learned. He does not know Romeo is on his way to the tomb with poison to die beside Juliet. His plan having miscarried, Laurence hopes to hide Juliet in his cell, send again to Romeo and then help the lovers escape. Overwhelmed by the passion of grief, however, Romeo rushes, in frantic despair, longing for death with the same passion with which he longs for Juliet, to the deadly conclusion of the play.

Not only is Romeo unaware of the truth of Juliet's death, he is also unaware of the plans to marry her to Paris, although after he kills Paris in the tomb he recalls that his servant had mentioned it to him but his "betossed soul did not attend him." Romeo is therefore surprised to find a man he does not know, for even as they fight he is unaware that Paris is his opponent, in Juliet's tomb performing rites which clearly, to him, are his own. Paris has come to lay flowers beside the corpse.

> Sweet flower, with flowers thy bridal bed I strew,—
> O woe! thy canopy is dust and stones;—
> Which with sweet water nightly I will dew,
> Or, wanting that, with tears distill'd by moans:
> The obsequies that I for thee will keep
> Nightly shall be to strew thy grave and weep.
>
> V.iii.12ff

Juliet dead serves Paris as well as Juliet living, perhaps better, for she no longer can frustrate his will for her to be his or his image of her. In either case, whether she is alive or dead, it is the idea of his possessing Juliet that Paris adores, not Juliet herself, whose own will is of no consequence to him. Throughout the play Paris courts Juliet only through conversations with her father. There is hardly an indication that Paris and Juliet even know each other. Actual contact between Juliet and Paris occurs only once in *Romeo and Juliet*, over an entirely unromantic twenty lines, when they meet, by accident, at Friar Laurence's cell.

Paris has come to Laurence to arrange the wedding ceremony for his marriage to Juliet. She has come ostensibly to make confession but actually to prevent the marriage and receive the fatal potion from the friar. Their conversation hardly reflects the speech of lovers. It is filled with Juliet's characteristic evasion and equivocation and shows Paris's overconfident will and assumption of formal possession of her. Her words have a different meaning to her from the meaning Paris attributes to them. That Paris is able to remain blind to Juliet's hardly veiled hostility shows he is guided only by his own will:

Paris: Happily met, my lady and my wife!
Juliet: That may be, sir, when I may be a wife.
Paris: That may be must be, love, on Thursday next.
Juliet: What must be shall be.

Laurence, in a fine display of his own duplicity, interjects what might seem a holy sentiment; but it is really an ironic equivocation that sets him clearly in Juliet's camp:

Friar Laurence: That's a certain text.

Paris is undaunted by, if he is even cognizant of, Juliet's iciness and their dialogue continues as it had begun:

Paris: Come you to make confession to this father?
Juliet: To answer that, I should confess to you.

Paris: Do not deny to him that you love me.
Juliet: I will confess to you that I love him.
Paris: So will ye, I am sure, that you love me.
Juliet: If I do so, it will be of more price,
Being spoke behind your back, than to your face.

Defeated in his attempt at familiarity, Paris tries gentleness, but Juliet is intractable. He again becomes proprietary, and she continues her equivocation:

Paris: Poor soul, thy face is much abused with tears.
Juliet: The tears have got small victory by that;
For it was bad enough before their spite.
Paris: Thou wrong'st it, more than tears, with that report.
Juliet: That is no slander, sir, which is a truth;
And what I spake, I spake it to my face.
Paris: Thy face is mine, and thou hast slander'd it.
Juliet: It may be so, for it is not mine own.

By which, of course, she means it belongs to Romeo. With that hidden rebuff, she turns to Laurence, "Are you at leisure, holy father, now;/ Or shall I come to you at evening mass?" saying not another word to Paris, leaving him alone with his unwanted gallantry. When he leaves, instead of saying good-bye to him, she says to Laurence, "O shut the door!" (IV.i.18ff)

Like Romeo at the beginning of the play, Paris in Juliet's tomb is a grieving lover consumed with a passion which feeds on his identity as a frustrated lover. He is interrupted in his lamentation by Romeo's arrival, however. Not knowing anymore than what is commonly thought, he thinks that Romeo "here is come to do some villainous shame/ To the dead bodies" of Juliet and Tybalt, who is also buried in the tomb of the Capulets.

As he had with Tybalt, so now Romeo tries to avoid Paris's challenge beginning with the words, "Good gentle youth, tempt not a desperate man;/ Fly hence, and leave me." Paris, like Tybalt, earlier, however, is insistent in his pursuit of what he considers honor and justice. "I do defy thy conjurations,/

And apprehend thee for a felon here," he replies. Like Tybalt, too, he is slain by Romeo. The play which had begun with a meaningless brawl and whose *peripeteia* was brought on by the vain duel between Tybalt and Mercutio ends with an absurd confrontation fueled by misinformed fury between Romeo and Paris.

Alone after killing Paris, Romeo utters the soliloquy, "How oft when men are at the point of death/ Have they been merry!" over Juliet's body as he prepares to take his own life. He is giddy. He wonders why he feels "A lightning before death," when he is going into a realm of darkness. As when he left Juliet's chamber on the morning after their wedding night, the meanings of light and darkness are here reversed. The same paradox occurs: the greater it grew light then, the deeper the darkness of exile was approaching. The more light he feels now the darker his grief as he endures the darkness of death. But the darkness of death, he notices next, has not descended yet on the corpse of Juliet and quenched her light. This brings forth in him mortuary poetry—sincere, lovely, and conventional, but subversive, too, of the convention, because it is false. When he asks conventionally,

Ah, dear Juliet,
Why art thou yet so fair? shall I believe
That unsubstantial death is amorous,
And that the lean abhorred monster keeps
Thee here in dark to be his paramour?

V.iii.101ff

the ironic answer is because she is alive, not dead. And when he declaims,

O my love! my wife!
Death, that hath suck'd the honey of thy breath,
Hath had no power yet upon thy beauty:
Thou art not conquer'd; beauty's ensign yet
Is crimson in thy lips and in thy cheeks,
And death's pale flag is not advanced there[,]

V.iii.90ff

it is not true because she is not dead. But death will conquer although, as Romeo speaks, its conquest has not yet been accomplished. It is he who now in haste and overwhelmed by the sense of defeated desire is death's workman.

Although Romeo delivers a long soliloquy before his death, Juliet, does not. She speaks directly even if sometimes with equivocation, as we have seen throughout the play, whether to other people, or, as in her first soliloquy on her balcony, if the other is not physically present, to herself. And she is not deceitful in her understanding. She analyzes things clearly, and she does not lie to herself, even if she does lie to others. She does not try to falsify reality or create an image of herself for herself. She is not deceived herself when she tries to deceive others, like her father. When she wakes, her mind is clear, "I do remember well where I should be,/ And there I am." (V.iii.149f) But things are not as they should be. "Where is my Romeo?" she asks of Friar Laurence who is beside her, having rushed to the tomb. "A greater power than we can contradict/ Hath thwarted our intents," (V.iii.153f) he tells her. It is a simple sentence, but it resonates deeply with the central theme of the harmful power of will: that a willful act subverts its own desired end.

> Thy husband in thy bosom there lies dead;
> And Paris too. Come, I'll dispose of thee
> Among a sisterhood of holy nuns.
>
> V.iii.155ff

But she refuses to follow. Hearing the noise of the watch approaching, Laurence flees the tomb. Caught in the rush of time and circumstance now, he actually has explained nothing to Juliet. But she understands well enough even without knowing the details of how things have happened, just what has happened, "a cup, closed in my true love's hand? Poison, I see, hath been his timeless end." Drawn to Romeo, as she has always been, and as he has been, even when he heard of her death, to her, unreflecting, she hastens after him:

.... I will kiss thy lips;
Haply some poison yet doth hang on them,
To make me die with a restorative.

V.iii.161ff

All that is left now is for the participants in the drama who have survived to gather and review the events which led to the catastrophe and to find some resolution. The noise in the tomb has brought the watch, the Prince, Old Montague—his wife has died of grief at Romeo's banishment—the Capulets, Romeo's man, and Paris's. Laurence is brought before them by the watch and quickly tells the story of the play, and that retelling of the story is the resolution of the story. Grief at their children's death seems to bring the old men to their senses and they end their enmity, each embracing the other's loss. For these fathers, death bestows on both the lovers mythic life as they are metamorphosed from living beings into frozen emblems of love. Rather than a thing of living passion, love becomes symbolic, figured forth in the golden statue each father will have sculpted of the other's child, not so much to represent the lovers as to represent the reconciliation both men have made with each other. The lovers' integrity of passion is denied them and they become in death emblems not of their own delight but of their fathers' will to reconciliation.

It remains for the Prince to recall the lovers themselves and the woeful context of their living love. Fittingly for a play about the strength of language and poetry in the construction and assertion of identity, a play which begins with a sonnet, and which uses a sonnet to represent the union of two lovers, the Prince ends the play with recognition of the lovers using the final sestet of a sonnet:

A glooming peace this morning with it brings;
The sun, for sorrow, will not show his head:
Go hence, to have more talk of these sad things;
Some shall be pardon'd, and some punished:
For never was a story of more woe
Than this of Juliet and her Romeo.

Notes

1. This and all other citations from the text refer to: Bryant, J.A., Jr., ed. *The Tragedy of Romeo and Juliet*. New York: New American Library, 1964.

2. http://absoluteshakespeare.com/guides/romeo_and_juliet/essay/romeo_and_juliet_essay.htm

Critical Views

JAMES C. BRYANT ON FRIAR LAURENCE AS A COMIC AND COMPROMISED ECCLESIASTIC

Shakespeare's England was particularly hostile to friars and other representatives of Roman Catholicism, especially following Philip's abortive invasion of 1588. Consequently, an original audience in 1594 was conditioned by years of political propaganda from pulpit, stage, and published works to recognize in Roman Catholic sentiment a political threat to England and to the Reformation.

(...)

An audience in 1594 would have been aware of the literary convention which often used friars and other ecclesiastics as the butt of ribald humor. In certain ways, as shall be pointed out later, Shakespeare seems to depict Friar Laurence in that long standing tradition of the comical friar dating backward in time to the songs of the Goliards, the medieval fabliaux, and the Italian *novellatori* which frequently made the religious, particularly the friars, subjects of their broad humor.[7]

(...)

Part of the difficulty modern readers have in assessing Friar Laurence objectively lies perhaps in an insistence upon seeing him with myopic focus as a sympathetic man with good intentions. At this point, however, an inherited romantic sympathy for the man should be distinguished from any completely objective consideration of the friar as an ecclesiastic. For to sympathize with him as a man must at the same time be to suspend his role as a religious, sequestered from ordinary secular engagement and devoted rather to a life of piety.

(...)

There yet remains the problem of judgment by a standard which the man necessarily renounces whenever he assumes the vows of an ecclesiastic. To judge the friar merely as a 'nextdoor neighbor' who has 'quite forgotten' his holy calling is to restore to him a status of carnality and secularism which he—and presumably the Church—would have found abhorrent. Indeed it is this disparity between *ought* and *is* that lay at the root of the comic tradition of friars in the fabliaux and in the bawdy tales of Boccaccio and Chaucer as well as in the contemporary drama. One must assume, then, that Shakespeare's audience would have seen Friar Laurence as one who *ought* to be 'ghostly sire' under the *regula* rather than as a 'nextdoor neighbor'. It is when he deviates from his spiritual function that he becomes problematic theologically.

(...)

If it is as an ecclesiastic that Friar Laurence's problematic character becomes most evident, it follows that his final judgment must be by the standards of canon low to which he is necessarily committed by irrevocable vows. In this regard a primary consideration should be the friar's apparent disregard of canon law forbidding clandestine marriages. Robert Stevenson points out that during the sixteenth century both Anglican and Roman Catholic canons forbade the clergy to perform secret marriages.[22] And, he states, to marry minors without parental knowledge or consent was considered a serious offence, incurring a penalty of suspension from clerical duties up to three years.[23] According to Stevenson, Brooke softened the offence by making Juliet sixteen years old, 'an age considered the minimum suitable one if we are to trust the most popular of the marriage manuals published in England by any of the Tudor printers'.[24]

(...)

That Shakespeare probably accepted sixteen as a minimum age may be inferred from Capulet's own words to Paris early in the play:

> My child is yet a stranger in the world—
> She hath not seen the change of fourteen years.
> Let two more summers wither in their pride
> Ere we may think her ripe to be a bride.
>
> (I.ii.8–11)

Nevertheless, Friar Laurence agrees to marry the lovers in the play without parental knowledge or consent and apparently in defiance of canon law forbidding clandestine marriage.

Before one can maintain that the 'sweet old man' was consistently the voice of wisdom in the drama, it may be a helpful corrective to recall that Brooke's friar was no obvious prevaricator: he merely told Juliet to take the potion home and drink it secretly. Shakespeare's Friar Laurence, however, causes Juliet to utter a deliberate lie in order to deceive her parents:

> Hold, then, go home, be merry, give consent
> To marry Paris.
>
> (Iv.i.89–90)

Moreover, the friar further deviates from what one would expect of the religious by becoming himself a prevaricator when he offers 'consolation' at Juliet's apparent death. Friar Laurence counsels the grieving parents not to mourn, for Juliet has 'advanced Above the clouds, as high as Heaven itself'.[28] One would expect that the function of the true is to speak truth. Indeed, in view of his questionable conduct in deviating from spiritual ideals, it would seem that only a romantic and sentimental argument can exonerate Friar Laurence from obvious deceit, hypocritical posing, and prevarication.

(...)

In view of the evidence it becomes difficult to insist upon the traditional interpretation of Shakespeare's friar as 'grave, wise, patient'. And Elizabethan audiences may have recognized in him the vestige of stage friars from the Middle Ages whose disparity between holy ideals and worldly actions were the substance of comic ridicule. This is not to suggest that Friar Laurence is the coarse comic figure of some of his fictional contemporaries, but the portrait we have of him often recalls some of those secular foibles and human weaknesses of which friars in literature were traditionally suspect—deceit, whim, carnality, or hypocrisy. Moreover, it is likely that a highly anti–Roman Catholic audience in 1594 would have viewed Friar Laurence's meddlesome activity in a secular love affair with less sympathy than would later audiences more distant from pervasive religious animosity. For although modern readers are inclined to pardon the friar upon the basis of his personal appeal, his good intentions, and primarily because he favors the young lovers, those perhaps less romantic must pass final judgment upon him as a cleric of dubious conduct. As such he appears not wise but impulsive, meddlesome in secular love affairs, deceitful to Juliet's parents, an equivocator, an instigator of prevarication, and apparently unfaithful to his canonical vows. Shakespeare makes him less the obvious stereotype of comical friars, but by discrediting his holy function in the drama the ultimate effect is similar: he is open in either case to ridicule. As a man he is inconstant and cowardly; as a cleric he is untrue to what his habit professes.

(...)

It is possible, then, that Friar Laurence is best understood as a part of the traditional comic spirit of the passionate love story which ends unhappily. His intentions are good but his hasty consent to unite the lovers in clandestine marriage and his poor judgment and problematic behavior in attempting to maintain the deception are at least partly responsible for the tragic consequences from which good intentions alone cannot exonerate him as a cleric. But with a callous disregard for the lovers, one can say that the friar's end to reconcile Capulet and

Montague has been successful, although at great cost. Moreover, since Shakespeare seems in some ways to discredit the cleric's ideal function by questionable conduct and doubtful means, one must consider the possibility that Friar Laurence's character in the drama is at least problematic and probably a mild derogation of friars in general according to commonplace Renaissance attitudes toward Roman Catholic clerics during the last decade of the sixteenth century. By understanding him in this way, Friar Laurence becomes in some significant ways the stereotype of the sly and meddlesome friar of the medieval literary tradition. That Shakespeare seemed to have something of this ancient tradition in mind can be inferred by his otherwise puzzling alterations of the friar from Brooke's poem. For, as it has been suggested earlier, Shakespeare's friar is less admirable, in some ways, and weaker than Brooke's. He is still real enough and sympathetically treated to a point, but he is seemingly deprived of those qualities one expects either in an admirable man or a dedicated clergyman. The result is a problematic figure who merits more than casual acceptance by traditional standards.

Notes

7. See Joseph S. Kennard, *The Friar in Fiction* (New York, 1923), p. 96.

22. Stevenson, p. 32. He cites for reference (as a 'fully documented discussion of clandestine marriage and its penalties') the *Encyclopédie Théologique*, IX (Paris, 1844), pp. 507–15.

23. Stevenson, p. 32. *See Constitutions and Canons 1604*, ed. H.A. Wilson (Oxford, 1923), Canon LXII, fol. Lz.

24. Stevenson, p. 32. His reference is to Henry Bullinger, *The Christen state of Matrymone*, trans. Miles Coverdale (London, 1552), fol. 16v. 'In ch. 5 he stated that any marriage without parental consent was void, founding his case on Scripture and the "Imperyall lawe". Bullinger's treatise was nine times reprinted before 1575. John Stockwood in 1589 published a 100-page treatise proving all marriages without parental consent to be null and void' (p. 49, n. 47).

28. In Brooke's poem the friar is not present at the 'death' scene of Juliet.

A number of questions (...) spring from the play when we bring to it questions of motivation. (...) The most interesting questions of motivation (...) center on Friar Lawrence. His prompt acquiescence to Romeo's wish to be married to Juliet and his failure to seek parental consent are puzzling acts. As an ecclesiastic he must have motive for defying canon laws that forbade clergy from performing secret marriages and that suspended for as many as three years any cleric who wed minors without parental knowledge or consent.[2] He must also have motive for refusing promptly to acquaint Prince Escalus with his plan to marry the young lovers and, thereby, to reconcile the feuding houses. And he must have motive for his elaborate, alchemical ruse. Why should he give Juliet a sleeping potion that requires her to deceive and bring grief, however disingenuous, to her family? Since the end he seeks is to reunite the couple and have Romeo take Juliet to Mantua, that end would be more simply served by spiriting her over the border.

(...)

Friar Lawrence (...) can be characterized, as is customary, to be a representative of moderation and wisdom.[3] But his stratagems and their aborted results also make it tempting to characterize him as a bungling priest, a hand-me-down from medieval fabliaux and *commedia erudita*.[4] Both characterizations, because they fail to examine carefully the question of motivation, overlook the more significant likelihood that Friar Lawrence is a duplicitous and ambitious man whose benevolent manner masks the political objectives of his deeds. Standing alongside the play's other "fathers," he seems as interested in his surrogate children, Romeo and Juliet, as Capulet is in his daughter, Juliet, and Prince Escalus is in his symbolic children, his Veronese citizens. But all three men—domestic father, civil monarch and religious benefactor—have strong political motivations. And the least suspect of the three, Friar Lawrence, is prompted by self-aggrandizing ambitions that are equal to, if not stronger than, those in Capulet and Prince Escalus.

(...)

First appearing in the play as a flower and herb gatherer, who could be more innocuous? Yet his analogy between a flower's poisonous and medicinal "Power" and man's "Two such opposed kings," "grace and rude will" (II.iii.27–28) tacitly acknowledges the existence in himself of "rude will" or, as we would call it now, libidinal and aggressive drives. Even more, his analogy, which develops the idea that every object has the ability to serve radically dissimilar ends, defines his mental habit of seeing power and conflicts of power all about him. Interestingly, he conceives of dawn as a victory of smiling morn over "frowning night," as a triumph of "Titan's [fiery] wheels" over drunkard-reeling darkness (1–4). He is impressed with earth's power to be both tomb and womb. And, as he registers, "mickle is the powerful grace that lies" in such inconspicuous, negligible, and insentient objects as "plants, herbs, stones" (15–16). In brief, Friar Lawrence's opening monologue is a hymn to power and to the uses and abuses to which it can be put. Aware that "Virtue itself turns vice, being misapplied,/ And vice sometime by action dignified" (21–22), the friar's relativism embellishes the theme that actions and motives are difficult to sound and discover. It also serves notice that he is capable of committing an act which, though it might appear a vice, could be dignified as a virtue.

(...)

Shakespeare begins to expose the political cunning of the friar by informing us what the friar chooses not to do, allowing us to infer the motives for such choices. Did the friar truly desire to halt the feud and turn "rancor to pure love," it seems probable that despite Romeo's plea "That thou consent to marry us to-

Gerry Brenner on a Dark View of Friar Lawrence's Motivations

day" (II.iii.64) the friar would seek out Montague or Capulet to receive parental consent and to determine whether the marriage would in fact bode "pure love." His refusal to seek either parent may testify to his knowledge of their implacable hatred and so to the futility of such a proceeding.[8] But it also testifies to the possibility that the friar desires to garner sole praise for finding a solution to the longstanding feud. Similarly, were the friar enamored of the idea of restoring civil order by means of a Montague–Capulet alliance, it seems probable that he would go directly to Prince Escalus, tell him what is afoot, and get his advice and approval. It is possible, of course, as with his refusal to seek audience with the parents, that ineptness or the press of clerical duties keeps him from such a visit. And Shakespeare may be following his source here. Brooke's friar, though a revered counsellor of the Prince, also fails to acquaint him with the marriage plans. But given Escalus' character, it is little wonder that Friar Lawrence chooses, I believe, not to go to him. If the friar sees him as I do, he would know that the insecure prince would resent the friar as a political threat whose plan would aggrandize the Church at the expense of the State. Or the friar would have cause to expect the prince to issue some imperious decree that would muddle his plan or cause him to compromise his commitment to Romeo. (Indeed if the prince knows that his kinsman Paris is courting Juliet, he would be particularly loath to endorse the friar's plan.)

By choosing to advise neither parents nor prince, the friar acts on his maxim that "Vice [is] sometime by action dignified." More significantly, his actions dramatize the rivalry between Church and State for power. The impotence of the domestic and civic "fathers" to arrest the feud and to restore harmony in the state creates the opportunity for a mere Franciscan friar to step into the breach. Consequently, the friar's actions betray the motive "so secret and so close" to his heart: to assert his superiority over domestic and civil authorities, to show that he can single-handedly solve the "ancient grudge," to demonstrate who the best father of Verona's welfare is.

(...)

The most telling proof of Friar Lawrence's political motivations is that he continually oversteps his ecclesiastical functions. By marrying Romeo and Juliet secretly and without parental consent, he knowingly violates strict canon law. He does so not to sanctify an act of Providence that has had Romeo and Juliet fall in love at first sight, but, as his express reason to Romeo indicates, "To turn your households' rancor to pure love." Acting on his own volition and interfering in temporal matters, the friar dramatizes the kind of behavior that so perplexes Capulet's illiterate servant. Trying to determine who is on his master's guest list, he remarks, "It is written that the shoemaker should meddle with his yard and the tailor with his last, the fisher with his pencil and the painter with his nets" (I.ii.39–41). To be sure, the friar is not alone in performing forbidden actions. Tybalt seems to thrive on proscribed behavior. Juliet quickly learns to defy parental dictates. And Romeo is a compulsive gate-crasher, trespassing and committing taboo acts throughout the play. The correlation between the behaviors of the friar and of other characters indicates that excepting Paris, defiance of conventional expectation is wholesale. The correlation also underscores the friar's refusal to abide by God's will. He prefers the autonomy of "My will be done." Taking an active role in the affairs of men, he shows his discontent with leaving matters in the hands of Providence. He even appropriates to himself the task of sending Romeo that crucial letter via a fellow friar, rather than let Romeo's servant, Balthasar, be his emissary, as he had promised Romeo he would (III.iii.169–71).

The friar's herbological interests align him with the play's other drugmaker, the apothecary who commits the outlawed act of selling poison to Romeo. But those interests are more tellingly the means by which Shakespeare has the friar flagrantly expose his urge for political preeminence. The clergy were, of course, usually conversant with simple natural medicine. And the friar's interest in alchemy surely has its beneficial aspect. But his chemical expertise shows that like many a scientific meddler, he tampers with God's natural order and uses nature's secret powers to serve his own purposes.

More specifically, on the pretext of restoring the lovers to each other, he tells a distraught Juliet that the ultimate consequence of her drinking his potion will be that Romeo will "bear thee hence to Mantua" (IV.i.117). But why is his alchemy necessary? Why not simply help Juliet flee Verona if he is genuinely interested in reuniting the lovers? His elaborate ruse requires that Juliet deceive her family, that they suffer unnecessary grief, and that he dissemble before them. More, his ruse tells us that he is less concerned with the lovers' happiness than with his ambition. That is, though the play never explicitly considers the question, it implicitly asks us to inquire: What would have happened had his ruse been successful?

Is my question beyond the scope of the play? I think not. After all, the recurrent motif of haste in the play sweeps the plot ever into the future. Capulet eagerly looks forward to Juliet's marriage, as does Paris. Prince Escalus eagerly looks forward to the day when the feud will be over. Romeo and Juliet eagerly look forward to being reunited. And Friar Lawrence eagerly looks forward, I believe, to a brilliant scenario. Had his ruse worked, he could have called for an audience with the prince—the Montagues and Capulets in attendance, naturally. Then he could have informed the Capulets that their daughter was not dead, as they thought, but was alive and happy. He could have explained that his sleeping potion—"(so tutored by my art)" (V.iii.243)—had made her appear dead. And he could have expected that Capulet would rejoice, just as he had after the friar had presumably taught Juliet to defer to his will and so to marry Paris: "My heart is wondrous light,/ Since this same wayward girl is so reclaim'd" (IV.ii.46–47). The friar could then have informed all present of the end that his resurrection scheme served: to end the feud and so restore civil harmony by marrying Romeo and Juliet. However humbly he might have divulged his gospel, its effect would be the same. He would receive civil adulation, such praise as Capulet had earlier accorded him: "Now, afore God, this reverend holy friar,/ All our whole city is much bound to him" (IV.ii.31–32). And such praise would vault the friar over the prince as Verona's miracle worker, its true leader.

(...)

Lying about his conduct in the tomb constitutes the friar's most contemptible, self-serving act because that act dishonors Juliet. He impugns her by falsely declaring that he "entreated her come forth/ and *bear this work of heaven with patience*" (260–61, emphasis added); his scant attendance in the tomb and his actual words to her give the lie to his statement. His reconstruction of the tomb scene shows his intent to portray her as an irrational, frenzied young bride, too impatient to listen to adult counsel. He maintains that "a noise," rather than his fear of being apprehended, "did scare me from the tomb" (262), implying that Juliet was too insensible to have heard any noises. And he insists that Juliet was "too desperate" to leave the tomb with him. Projecting upon her his oven desperation, he once again attempts to deny her the measure of composure that is dramatically necessary for her to possess if she is to be accorded the dignity of the tragic heroine that I believe she has. While Juliet's last speech is certainly open to interpretation, I find in it the awareness, sense of responsibility, and composure that permit her a rightful claim to tragic stature. But the friar, interested in his own skin and image, as well as in concealing his political ambitions, will disallow her claim.

My reading of Friar Lawrence should offer more than just a different view of his character. It should show the friar's relationship to the political interests of the other two father figures in the play, a relationship that augments the play's conflict between the authorities of politics and of love. This in turn should enrich the play's emotional force by undercutting the potential melodrama that lies in the apparent collision of a bad father, Capulet, and a good father, Friar Lawrence. My reading also emphasizes the discrepancy between the play's irresponsible or ineffective adults and those responsible adolescents who, I believe, fully accept the consequences of their actions. Finally, it sees *Romeo and Juliet* conforming to an interest that long preoccupied Shakespeare. Whether we look to the history plays that precede *Romeo and Juliet*, to companion plays like *Midsummer's Night's Dream*, or to the more mature tragedies that follow, we find Shakespeare ever attentive to the subtleties, deceptions, finesses, failures, and problems that the desire for power, especially political power, can generate. To fail to see him attending to subtle power politics in this early tragedy underestimates his genius and ignores one of his most pervasive concerns.

Notes

2. Robert Stevenson, *Shakespeare's Religious Frontier* (The Hague: M. Nijhoff, 1958), p. 32.

3. For one among the many voices which articulate this customary view, see G.B. Harrison, *Shakespeare: The Complete Works* (New York: Harcourt, 1952), p. 6.

4. James C. Bryant, "The Problematic Friar in *Romeo and Juliet*," *English Studies*, 55 (1974), 340–50, offers a healthy antidote to the conventional view of Friar Lawrence.

8. Philip Traci, "Religious Controversy in *Romeo and Juliet*: The Play and Its Historical Context," *Michigan Academician*, 8 (1976), 319–25, argues the play's conflict between Catholics and Jews; consequently, Friar Lawrence would not seek audience with Capulet, the father of "the little Jewess," Juliet.

RUDOLF STAMM ON THE INTEGRATION OF SPEECH AND ACTION

No observer of Shakespeare's tragedy can fail to notice the importance of the first meeting of the lovers. It constitutes the climax prepared by the preceding scenes of Act 1, and, in the structure of the whole play, it is—like Romeo's fateful duel with Tybalt and the death scene—one of the turning points. It is the event that changes Romeo's and Juliet's lives, bringing them intense happiness at first and suffering and death in consequence. Shakespeare used all the resources of his rapidly developing art to provide this decisive encounter with a very special kind of dramatic life, moulding the first exchange of his young lovers into the form of a sonnet, of which he knew himself a master. To go with it he chose imagery also derived from the Petrarchan tradition with its tendency to express love in religious terms. And he saw to it that this poetic inset did not remain a literary exercise by integrating it in a dramatic event with its specific movements and gestures. As a result he achieved a unique combination of formality and spontaneity, of elegance and intensity, of wit and passion. Its impact is felt by every reader, performer or spectator, but to analyse and explain it has proved a difficult task for the critics. In their discussions they have often been struck by one or the other of its qualities only and overlooked or played down other aspects.

(...)

We (...) begin our own study of the meeting by recalling what we have learnt concerning the destined lovers in the preceding scenes. We have become better acquainted with Romeo than with Juliet. From the beginning he appears different from his cheerful friends, absorbed as he is by his Petrarchistic cult of an ideal and ideally inaccessible mistress. In fact, he avoids the contacts with reality and with other people as much as possible, and what we hear from Benvolio and old Montague of his tearful morning walks to the sycamore grove and the self-sought confinement in his darkened room reminds us of a figure in a tapestry representing scenes from the *Roman de la Rose*. His absence from the first street brawl shows how far he has withdrawn from the normal life of his friends. When he makes his entry we are struck by the abundance of his fanciful love rhetoric and his poverty of significant gestures. His references to his actual surroundings are weak and merely *pro forma*.[9]

(...)

When the ball begins Juliet has remained a less clearly defined figure than Romeo. (...) When Lady Capulet wants to know her thoughts about marriage and then, quite specifically, about Count Paris as a suitor, her answers are obedient, but also quite noncommittal. In fact, her reply to her mother's brusque main question shows that she can easily compete with the young gentlemen out of doors in the arts of ornate speech and punning and that she is mistress of the diplomatic if-sentence:

I'll look to like, if looking liking move,
But no more deep will I endart mine eye
Than your consent gives strength to make it fly.
(I.iii.97–9)

Another hint that she is by no means a naive child but a young lady with her wits about her is given where she manages to stop the nurse's overwhelming flow of words by capping her repeated 'it stinted, and said "Ay"' by an energetic: 'And stint thou too, I pray thee, Nurse, say I.' (58)

(...)

In the ball scene Juliet enters with the rest of the Capulets and obeys her father's urgent invitation to dance. Romeo, one of the young masquers welcomed by Capulet, disregards this invitation, sticking to his decision to stand aside and watch. He sees Juliet and is struck by her beauty:
What lady's that which doth enrich the hand
Of yonder knight? (I.v.41f.)
His as yet half-conscious desire to touch her hand himself manifests itself in a discreet demonstrative gesture and in the metaphor 'enrich her hand'. Too busy to listen properly, the servant addressed gets rid of the untimely questioner by a bare 'I know not, sir'. Romeo does not insist since he is getting more and more absorbed by the vision before him.

(...)

Romeo approaches, doffs his masque, kneels before Juliet, touches and gently raises her hand offering to kiss it. The effects of this first tender touch, described by Baumgart with so much empathy, make themselves felt. A wave of delight overcomes him, but it cannot render the hero of an early play by Shakespeare speechless. He speaks before the intended kiss and, in order to tame his emotions, he chooses the demanding form of a cross-rhymed quatrain for his first address:

If I profane with my unworthiest hand
This holy shrine, the gentle sin is this:
My lips, two blushing pilgrims, ready stand
To smooth that rough touch with a tender kiss. (92–5)

It is difficult for him to find words and images for the message which has passed from hand to hand with the most convincing urgency. His perturbation is great, and the playwright has seen to it that it leaves its marks on his deceptively smooth lines. Two of them are outstanding. The first is the half-line 'the gentle sin is this', a fragment of a thought, not directly connected with the properly organized sentence that precedes and follows it. Romeo cannot be fully coherent at this moment, breathless and passionate as he is. The dramatic significance of this loose bit of speech has escaped too many editors and critics. Their blindness to it has sent them on a vain chase after emendations or fine-spun explanations trying to make sense of what is not meant to make sense. Another sign of Romeo's turmoil appears in the awkwardness of the imagery in the second part of his quatrain. For a moment the old self-absorbed acolyte of the artificial cult of love asserts himself again in the narcissistic and almost grotesque comparison of his lips to two blushing pilgrims.

We now approach the most decisive and moving moment in this love encounter. So much depends upon Juliet's reaction to Romeo's appeal. With spontaneous empathy she senses his predicament, but she notices his blunders, too. What she says in a quatrain of her own is beyond anything he could have hoped for:

Good pilgrim, you do wrong your hand too much,
Which mannerly devotion shows in this;

> For saints have hands that pilgrims' hands do touch,
> And palm to palm is holy palmers' kiss. (96–9)

It is difficult to do justice to everything she achieves in these words with great ease and naturalness. She enters into the imaginative scene that Romeo has begun to enact—not quite successfully in consequence of his excitement. She corrects his mistakes and distributes the roles in it properly: For the part of the pilgrim she casts, not the lips of the lover kneeling in front of her, but himself, and for herself she accepts the role, not of an impersonal shrine, but of a personal saint. She quickly withdraws her hand from his, thus refusing the kiss he intended to place on it. This is not done from coyness or shyness, but because her own emotions tell her that a kiss on her hand is no longer enough. So she induces a different development of the playlet in which they are now both passionately engaged. To speak here of scheming and calculation would betray a poorish way of seeing things. The fact is that the girl proves herself more mature than the boy; she takes control of the situation and is able not only to mend Romeo's speech, but to perfect the love that has sprung up in both of them.

In order to understand what is happening to the lovers now we should remember John Keats's version of the Romeo and Juliet theme. At the critical moment in *The Eve of St. Agnes*, Porphyro is able to enter into Madeline's dream of love,[11] a consummation so absolute that the couple cease being human and mortal as they glide by all the obstacles in their way out of the castle into another world of myth and legend. Juliet's perfect response to Romeo's appeal corresponds to Porphyro's passing into Madeline's dream. What happens after the decisive event takes a few minutes in the poem and a few days in the play, but Shakespeare's lovers cannot simply glide away from reality and life; their sufferings and their deaths become as real as their ecstatic happiness.

On hearing Juliet's reply Romeo does not misinterpret the withdrawal of her hand. He feels how completely she is with him, and therefore his bewilderment leaves him at once. He jumps to his feet and boldly asks: 'Have not saints lips, and holy palmers too?' As he tries to embrace her they allow free play to their passionate wit and are carried by it to the immense satisfaction of their first kiss:

> **Juliet**: Ay, pilgrim, lips that they must use in prayer.
> **Romeo**: O then, dear saint, let lips do what hands do:
> They pray: grant thou, lest faith turn to despair.
> **Juliet**: Saints do not move, though grant for prayer's sake.
> **Romeo**: Then move not, while my prayer's effect I take.
>
> (100–5)

As the kiss unites the lovers, the sonnet, the form they have chosen for their coming together, is complete. They should stop now, but their youthful vehemence and desire for another kiss drive them on through an excessive quatrain:

> **Romeo**: Thus from my lips, by thine, my sin is purg'd.
> **Juliet**: Then have my lips the sin that they have took.
> **Romeo**: Sin from my lips? O trespass sweetly urg'd.
> Give me my sin again.
> **Juliet**: You kiss by th' book. (106–9)

The delight they take in each other betrays them into this anticlimax. As they expand the sonnet their wit becomes more quibbling than before, and Juliet herself is critical of it in her final remark. Behind the fun of going on beyond the limits of the sonnet and of wringing further effect out of its imagery the hint is lurking that this new-born love is too violent to respect forms and conventions and that the excess in it might prove dangerous. Before embarking on the third quatrain the couple may well be lightly touched by the consciousness of this and hesitate a moment, and the words 'Thus from my lips, by thine, my sin is purg'd' may come somewhat hesitatingly from Romeo's lips. It cannot be more than the passing of a white cloud announcing the darker ones which crowd in upon the lovers when they seek and obtain information concerning each other's name and family at the end of the scene. The recognition of what has happened to them makes Romeo cry out:

Is she a Capulet?
O dear account. My life is my foe's debt. (116f.)

Soon this will be echoed by Juliet's

My only love sprung from my only hate.
Too early seen unknown, and known too late.
Prodigious birth of love it is to me
That I must love a loathed enemy. (137–40)

When the curious nurse wants to know what she is talking about Juliet's sly answer is subtly balanced between banter and wistfulness:

A rhyme I learn'd even now
Of one I danc'd withal. (141f.)

Again her *savoir faire* reminds us of that early maturity which stood her in such good stead when she had to cope with Romeo's first blundering address.

It has been our aim in this essay to show how intimately the sonnet is connected with the gestic events of the meeting scene and how much the importance of its dramatic functions outweighs the decorative ones.

Notes

9. All quotations are taken from the *Arden Edition* of the play by Brian Gibbons.

11. *Cf. The Eve of St. Agnes*, Stanza XXXVI.

SUSANNA GREER FEIN ON HERBS AND ROMANCE

Friar Lawrence's knowledge of the secret properties ("virtues") of herbs underscores a dramatic premise of *Romeo and Juliet*, namely that good intent often intermixes with ill effect, and vice versa: "Virtue itself turns vice, being misapplied,/ And vice sometime by action dignified" (2.3.21–22). In a drama of tragic design in which crossed human affairs are analogous to the impartial operation of substance in the natural world, some characters' names are linked suggestively to specific herbs and their intrinsic virtues: Romeo with rosemary (2.4.211–12)[1] and either Lady Capulet or the Nurse with angelica (4.4.5–6; see Ferguson and Yachnin; Bate). A previously unnoticed allusion to a plant and its traditional properties appears, too, in the name of Count Paris. Herb paris carried a centuries-old tradition of popular moralization in English writings. Any Elizabethan playgoer who remembered that herb paris was the familiar English true love plant would probably have recognized the relevance of its general import.

Although the name Paris occurs in both English and non-English texts prior to Shakespeare (Moore 99, 115–17), only Shakespeare appears to have worked the name into the symbolism of plants that informs his version of the romantic tragedy. Because of the truelove's distinctive name and shape, the herb became the mediating metaphor for numerous late-medieval poems and sermons on the subject of the opposition between secular and spiritual love. A poet with Shakespeare's wide-ranging eye and ear for detail could hardly have avoided the fitting comparisons offered by Paris's herbal namesake.

The plant's botanical name is *Paris quadrifolia*, but it went by the regional names "four-leaved grass," "truelove," "true love's knot," and "true lover's knot." From medieval records it is clear that these English terms reflected popular meanings attached to the plant, especially the connotation of faithfulness in love (translated by Shakespeare into Count Paris's cloying persistence). The plant's four equal leaves also led to its being widely taken as a sign of the cross, with an assortment of ensuing religious analogies; the plant's earliest recorded name, from the thirteenth century, is *Crux Christi* (von Schroff 3–4). The botanical term *paris* derives from Latin *pars*, "equal," a description of the leaves. Gerard, the author of a popular Elizabethan herbal (1597), hints that specimens of the plant were commonly likened to both crosses and truelove knots:

Herbe Paris riseth up with one small tender stake two hands high; at the very top whereof come forth route leaves directly set one against another in manner of a Burgundian Crosse or True-love knot: for which cause among the Antients it hath been called Herbe True-love. (101)

Aspirant lovers would adorn themselves with the plant for good luck. The tradition is recorded succinctly in a proverbial rhyme from the fourteenth century:

Trewe-loue among men that most is of lette,
In hattes, in hodes, in porses is sette.
Trewe-loue in herbers spryngeth in May.
Bote trewe loue of herte went is away.

This verse was set down, apparently from a popular source, by an English Franciscan, in a handbook for preachers, the *Fasciculus Morum* (Wenzel 159–60). The first line puns upon the name: truelove—a plant fastened upon hats, hoods, and purses—is the quality among men that is most fallible ("of lette"). Though trueloves grow abundantly in Maytime gardens, in human hearts the quality does not last. The proverb attests to a country fashion of bearing the plant upon one's person. In *The Miller's Tale* Chaucer makes humorous use of the practice by having Absolon, the ludicrous would-be lover, place a "trewelove" under his tongue in anticipation of stealing a kiss (I.3692).

The *Fasciculus Morum* verse demonstrates more than an English village fashion, however; it also illustrates the didactic use of the plant by medieval preachers: herb paris represents the transience of earthly love. The oft-repeated message was that such love is not to be trusted; one should look instead to true spiritual love of God. Herb paris becomes an earthly emblem of love that paradoxically asks us to abandon it and search for perfect love in a spiritual realm. Taking this tradition quite seriously, a contemporary of Chaucer wrote the alliterative *Quatrefoil of Love* on an elaborate conceit of herb paris likened (and contrasted) to God's true love exemplified in the events of the cross.

In the mirror-like oppositions that exist between Paris and Romeo,[2] Shakespeare sets up a contrast between mundane, earthly love and sublime union in love, a contrast that echoes the moralizations on herb paris as an embodiment of the ephemeral love that fades and as an emblem of the heavenly love to which one ought to aspire. Early in the play Lady Capulet speaks of Paris to Juliet as the finest flower of Verona's summer (1.3.77), a sentiment echoed by the Nurse: "Nay, he's a flower, in faith, a very flower" (78). In the context of the truelove tradition, this comparison becomes something more than simple praise: although beautiful, summer flowers such as Count Paris will always wither, offering a comfort that is merely temporary.

Paris eventually represents a shallow love offered to Juliet in her everyday, familial, public life, a love that ordinarily would seem desirable and even happy. But, like the summer flowers that Count Paris bears to Juliet's tomb (5.3.9, 12), such love dies with time. Romeo, whose name connotes for Juliet the herb rosemary, or remembrance (Williams 402–03), offers her an escape from such an ordinary existence.[3] Taken together, the male suitors' roles dramatize love in two forms, each an inversion of the other, with a strong reminiscence of medieval moralizations on earthly versus spiritual love. Their alternating presence upon the stage renders them virtually unknown to each other, at least, that is, until Paris's death in the last scene, an event that allows their symbolic paths momentarily to intersect and Romeo to recognize his rival (5.3.75). Yet even in death Paris's love remains but a weak shadow of Romeo's. In stark contrast to Paris's simple floral token, the items borne by Romeo to Juliet's tomb are poison and a dagger, symbols of a marriage that will be eternalized in death.

Given the general import of herb lore elsewhere in the play, these many points of resemblance between Paris and the traditional "virtues" of herb paris can only, I think, be understood as Shakespeare's quaint signal to Paris's character. Count Paris is fated to be no more than a summer flower, his death in Juliet's tomb fading from the playgoer's memory, while Romeo's dying for love achieves a dimension of immortality.

Notes

1. Traditionally used at weddings and at funerals, rosemary carries a paradoxical valence in the play; its dual properties coalesce when the Capulets' wedding preparations turn to mourning (4.5.89–90). On the rosemary theme, see especially Williams 400–03: also Hartwig 82–84 and Smith 579–83. On flower imagery in general, see Toole 26.

2. Other ways in which Shakespeare developed a dramatic opposition between Romeo and Paris are explored by Newman and Williams 13–19. Some of their interpretations are doubtful, however, especially that "all three marry in the same instant" in the tomb (16) and that Paris is Romeo's "younger self" (18). Harry Levin justly perceives that Paris carries "an aspect of unreality" (5). Other critics comment only in passing upon Paris's minor role; see, for example, Kahn 99–100 ("dull and proper"); Dickey 113 ("perhaps a stuffy fellow," but "quite right legally"); Hartwig 108–10 (a final reminder of the play's "feuding principle" and that Romeo has matured); and Moisan 142 ("a talisman of [Romeo's] theoretical victory over ... Death"). On the waste of Paris's death, see Rozett 157.

3. For related discussions of the theme of love, see Siegel and also Vyvyan 160–61.

Works Cited

Bate, A. Jonathan. "An Herb by Any Other Name: *Romeo and Juliet*, V.iv.5–6." *Shakespeare Quarterly* 33 (1982): 336.

Brooke, Arthur. *Tragicall Historye of Romeus and Juliet*. In *Romeo and Juliet*. Ed. G. Blakemore Evans. The New Cambridge Shakespeare. Cambridge: Cambridge UP. 1984. 213–47.

Chaucer, Geoffrey. *The Riverside Chaucer*. Gen. ed. Larry D. Benson. Boston: Houghton-Mifflin, 1974.

Dickey, Franklin M. *Not Wisely But Too Well: Shakespeare's Love Tragedies*. San Marino, CA: Huntington Library, 1966.

Ferguson, Liane, and Paul Yachnin. "The Name of Juliet's Nurse." *Shakespeare Quarterly* 32 (1981): 95–96.

Gerard, John. *Gerard's Herbal: The History of Plants*. Ed. Marcus Woodward. Rpt. London: Senate (Studio Editions), 1994.

Hartwig, Joan. *Shakespeare's Analogical Scene: Parody as Structural Syntax*. Lincoln: U of Nebraska p, 1983.

Kahn, Coppelia. *Man's Estate: Masculine Identity in Shakespeare*. Berkeley: U of California P, 1981.

Levin, Harry. "Form and Formality in *Romeo and Juliet*." *Shakespeare Quarterly* 11 (1960): 3–11.

Moisan, Thomas. "Shakespeare's Chaucerian Allegory: The Quest for Death in *Romeo and Juliet* and the Pardoner's Tale." *Chaucerian Shakespeare: Adaptation and Transformation*. Eds. E. Talbot Donaldson and Judith J. Kollmann. Detroit: Michigan Consortium for Medieval and Early Modern Studies, 1983. 131–49.

Moore, Olin H. *The Legend of Romeo and Juliet*. Columbus: Ohio State UP, 1950.

Newman, Paula, and George Walton Williams. "Paris: The Mirror of Romeo." *Renaissance Papers* 1981 (1982): 13–19.

The Quatrefoil of Love. Eds. Israel Gollancz and Magdalene M. Qeale. Early English Text Society, o.s. 195. Rpt. Millwood, NY: Kraus, 1971.

Rozett, Martha Tuck. "The Comic Structures of Tragic Endings: The Suicide Scenes in *Romeo and Juliet* and *Antony and Cleopatra*." *Shakespeare Quarterly* 36 (1985): 152–64.

Shakespeare, William. *The Riverside Shakespeare*. Gen. ed. G. Blakemore Evans. Boston: Houghton, 1974.

Siegel, Paul N. "Christianity and the Religion of Love in *Romeo and Juliet*." *Shakespeare Quarterly* 12 (1961): 371–92.

Smith, Warren D. "Romeo's Final Dream." *Modern Language Review* 62 (1967): 579–83.

Toole, William B. "The Nurse's 'Vast Irrelevance': Thematic Foreshadowing in *Romeo and Juliet*." *South Atlantic Bulletin* 45 (1980): 21–30.

von Schroff, Carl. *Historische Studie über Paris Quadrifolia*. Graz: Leuschner & Lubensky, 1890.

Vyvyan, John. *Shakespeare and the Rose of Love*. London: Chatto & Windus, 1960.

Wenzel, Siegfried. *Verses in Sermons: 'Fasciculus Morum' and Its Middle English Poems*. Cambridge: The Medieval Academy of America, 1978.

Williams, Phillip. "The Rosemary Theme in *Romeo and Juliet*." *Modern Language Notes* 68 (1953): 400–03.

Romeo and Juliet, the story of "star-crossed" love, is so well and
so deeply rooted in a number of traditions—those of myth,
legend, folklore, novella, to name a few—that to present it as a
subversive play may appear paradoxical and perhaps even
perverse. Yet the play's main polarities that explore the frictions
between high and low spheres, public and private lives, age and
youth, authority and rebellion, sacred and secular love,
generate powerful whirls of energy that partly account for its
enduring fascination for world audiences.

(...)

The very genre of the play—a love tragedy—is itself a
subversion of tragedy since the first two acts correspond to the
structure of Shakespearean comedy until Mercutio is turned
into a "grave man," thus causing the play to veer off into
tragedy. Gender is also subverted, as Shakespeare plays at
presenting an active, almost masculine Juliet against a weak,
effeminate Romeo.

The law is subverted by a love that brings about a
destabilization of domestic order, thus leading to a world where
contraries are reconciled in a series of sublime or grotesque
conjunctions (high and low, hate and love, the sacred and the
profane, life and death) so as to create a series of discordant
fusions.

(...)

Young Shakespeare seems to have delighted in delineating the
ravages of misrule, of the hurly-burly of love and desire, in a
traditional aristocratic society dominated by custom,
patriarchy, and well-established wealth.[1] Festivity is not limited
to orchestrating the coming of age in Verona or the various
rites of passage for young men and women, but it also serves to
turn the world upside down, to subvert its rigid hierarchies.

United with the subversive power of love, festivity does not only achieve a temporary suspension of social rules and political authority, but it also leads to a radical questioning of traditional patriarchal order.

(...)

In the play's dialectics, love is a transcending force that disrupts and subverts the marriage strategies of the establishment but it is itself subverted by Mercutio's wit and by the Nurse's bawdy humor. In creating a multiplicity of perspectives, Shakespeare is able to view the central love story from conflicting and parallel lines and thus to deflate some of its potential pathos and sentimentality. Romanticism is pitted against the cynical view of love as sex, as an affair of a "poperin pear" in an "open arse" (2.1.38), as Mercutio crudely puts it. The voices of tradition and subversion are not one-sided in this play but constantly interact and reflect one another so that they oblige the spectator and the reader to resort to constant realignments of perspective. We find a similar dynamic at the level of social, sexual, and gender roles, as well as of ideological positions in general.

(...)

An (...) example of the subversion of the ordinary opposition between life and death may be found in the scene where Juliet is discovered dead on the morning of her marriage to Count Paris. The hysterical nature and the hyperbolic artificiality of the collective lamentations orchestrated by the Nurse and articulated by Old Capulet have often been rightly pointed out. This is all the more visible as the audience knows that Juliet is not actually dead, so that all emotion is drained of the lament and mourning is turned into a hollow performance. As Thomas Moisan writes:

> Shakespeare deliberately undercuts the rhetoric of grief in this scene to underscore, by contrast, the more genuine

emotions of Romeo and Juliet ... the ululant effusions of the mourners, with their "O"-reate apostrophes and expletives undeleted ... are too "high" and "tragic" for a death that has not actually occurred, while the punning *badinage* between Peter and the musicians is too "low" and "comic" for a death that is *supposed* to have occurred.... [30]

So when Paris expresses his grief by exclaiming,

Beguil'd, divorced, wronged, spited, slain.
Most detestable Death, by thee beguil'd,
By cruel, cruel thee quite overthrown
(4.5.55–58)

he follows suit and amplifies Capulet's most vocal lamentation but he also unwittingly reveals that Romeo, who has taken Juliet away from him and married her in secret, is now identified with the figure of Death. He had already been recognized as such by Tybalt during the masque scene in 1.5, when the latter had described him as "cover'd with an antic face" (the word *antic*, as *Richard II* reveals, was a traditional name for death).[31] So, among the play's supreme ironies and successive reversals we discover that the two rivals for Juliet's love, both unknown to each other, are allowed to be cheated and defeated by a false death. This is the result of Friar Laurence's unfortunate attempt to simulate death to preserve life, which led him to a dangerous transgression with unforeseen consequences.

The subversion of the border between life and death at the initiative of figures that seem hallmarked by tradition and experience follows another subversion, namely that of gender roles in the play. This appears when Romeo compares Juliet with the sun in the "balcony" scene:

But soft, what light through yonder window breaks?
It is the east and Juliet is the sun!
Arise fair sun and kill the envious moon
Who is already sick and pale with grief

That thou her maid art far more fair than she.
(2.2.2–6)

Juliet is placed above him and Romeo hears her from below, unseen in the dark. He is thus spatially dominated by Juliet and this places him in an inferior, passive position, later acknowledged by Romeo himself when he describes the situation in terms of the mystic adoration of a saint:

> O speak again bright angel, for thou art
> As glorious to this night, being o'er my head,
> As is a winged messenger of heaven
> Unto the white-upturned wondering eyes
> Of mortals that fall back to gaze on him
> When he bestrides the lazy-puffing clouds
> And sails upon the bosom of the air.
> (2.2.26–32; emphasis mine)

Juliet, compared to an angel, is made explicitly masculine here, riding the clouds in the air like the incubus Queen Mab in Mercutio's description "the hag, when maids lie on their backs,/ That presses them and learns them first to bear" (1.5.92–93).[32] Furthermore, Romeo is said to be "fishified" by love—that is, emasculated: Mercutio says that he has lost his "roe" and compares him to a "dried herring," an image evoking Lenten fare (2.4.38–39). After Mercutio's death, Romeo will indeed exclaim:

> O sweet Juliet,
> Thy beauty hath made me effeminate
> (3.1.115–16)

Critics have also noted that it is Juliet who is allowed to speak the prothalamic soliloquy in 3.2 ("Gallop apace, you fiery-footed steeds"), thus reversing the traditional sexual roles, since the prothalamion was traditionally sung by the bridegroom on the eve of the marriage night. This detail adds to Juliet's self-confidence, turning her into what a critic has called an "atypical, unblushing, eager bride."[33] The last line of the play, which reverses the order of the appearance of the heroes in the title—"For never was a story of more woe/ Than this of Juliet and *her* Romeo"—making Romeo the one who belongs to Juliet rather than the other way around, cannot only express the necessities of the rhyme. It also confirms the subversion of traditional sexual relations and the taking over of initiative and authority by Juliet in the field of love and sex.

The love between the two children of enemy families leads to a reversal of ordinary social and sexual roles and to the subversion of the borders between life and death. The initial transgression lies in the love at first sight experienced during the masque at old Capulet's house, and it will subsequently defeat all the plans worked out by the traditional forces and voices of authority in the play (parents, confessor, Nurse). Paradoxically, the speeches that remind us of times past, of grave customs and ancient power, are laden with ironical foreboding of the inevitable transgression and subversion of tradition that will be allowed to take place. The subversion of life by death is itself an old idea found in morality plays, and it is mainly due to its being placed in a Renaissance context and applied to a pair of young and innocent lovers that it may be regarded as sensational or shocking. More intriguing is the ambiguous game played with the idea and the gruesome representation of death itself, which is responsible for the creation of horror with a sort of morbid, pre-Gothic or even Poesque thrill.[34] The repeated occurrences of the normally rather rare figure of the oxymoron serve to "define the carnal knowledge of a love in which life and death intertwine"[35] and this macabre representation is (given pride of place, often with a highly visual emphasis, in important soliloquies (4.3.15–58 and 5.3.75–120).

(...)

Tradition in *Romeo and Juliet* is certainly seen as a constraint that reduces the freedom of the individuals,[37] obliging them to follow the inherited hatreds of the clannish feud, "the continuance of their parents' rage," as the sonnet Prologue puts it, rather than gratify their own inclinations. On the other hand, the importance or the precedence given to tradition also implies that there is an obligation inherent in ceremony, a respect due to the laws of hospitality that, for instance, leads Old Capulet to curb Tybalt's fury when he recognizes Romeo hiding behind his "antic face" in the ball scene (1.5.53–91).

But Shakespeare treats the whole relation in a more complex, dialectic manner, as tradition in the play combines order and disorder, discipline and disobedience (to the Prince and to the laws of Verona). Moreover, characters like the Nurse and the Friar, who represent the voices of tradition, engage in soliloquies full of subversive potential. Their various attitudes and actions in the play also favor the clandestine resistance of the lovers to their family traditions. Does not Friar Laurence, after all, go far beyond the allowed limits of the church tradition and of his own responsibility as a holy man when he tampers with the forces of life and death and allows Juliet to "continue two and forty hours" in a "borrow'd likeness of shrunk death" (4.2.105–6)? Mercutio is also a highly ambiguous figure who embodies the traditional cynicism of young men's festive societies while simultaneously allowing the darker forces of dream, desire, and death to haunt his eerie Queen Mab soliloquy (1.4.53–94).

By contrasting and combining the voices of tradition and the forces of subversion in his early love tragedy, Shakespeare was in fact still experimenting with the power of dramatic art. Even if the influence of Marlowe is still very much felt in this play, the lovers pay a heavy price in the end and they cannot be said to be "overreachers" like Tamburlaine or Doctor Faustus. They do not set out to conquer the world or engage in black arts and in the quest of forbidden knowledge. They do not pay for their own sins only (impatience, anger, and revolt) or for their own blindness or naiveté, but they are also the victims of the subversive forces let loose by some of the other characters in the play (the Nurse, Mercutio, and Friar Laurence). Their love heroism is certainly misguided and vulnerable, as the recurrent imagery of the tempest-tossed or pilotless ship suggests,[38] but it also reflects the contradictions and clashes in Verona's patriarchal system as well as those inside the world of desire itself.

In the last analysis, their death is the sign of a triumph of sterility over the hope for continuity and regeneration, since it is not the old who die in the play, as tradition and natural laws would have it, but mainly the young (Mercutio, Tybalt, Paris, Romeo, and Juliet). The golden statues raised by the parents to commemorate the two eponymous heroes in the end are a sad and painful tribute, a mourning monument built to remind future generations of the dangers of civil strife and of the triumph of tradition over individual desire with its subversive potential. But, as the play itself plainly shows, this Pyrrhic victory is just another name for disaster since it is achieved at considerable expense, that of the sacrifice of the young and of the forces of life and renewal.

Notes

1. In a study of the early plays, Alexander Leggatt pits Shakespeare's well-known "sense of control" (as illustrated by the tightly knit structure of *A Midsummer Night's Dream*) against what he rightly calls "a fascination with the anarchic" (Alexander Leggatt, *English Drama: Shakespeare to the Restoration, 1590–1660* [London: Longman, 1988], 31).

30. "Rhetoric and the Rehearsal of Death: the 'Lamentations' Scene in *Romeo and Juliet*," *Shakespeare Quarterly* 34 (1983): 390.

31. *Romeo and Juliet* 1.5.55. See Laroque, "'Cover'd with an Antic Face': Les masques de la lumière et de l'ombre, " 390.

32. In this connection see Ann Lecercle, "Winking in *Romeo and Juliet*," in *Roméo et Juliette: Nouvelles perspectives critiques*, ed. Maguin and Whitworth, 259.

33. Whittier, "The Sonnet's Body and the Body Sonnetized in *Romeo and Juliet*, " 33.

34. See Mario Praz, *The Romantic Agony* (1933; reprint, Oxford: Oxford University Press, 1991), 27–32.

35. Whittier, "The Sonnet's Body, " 32.

37. At a lecture at the Sorbonne Nouvelle in November 1992, Brian Gibbons spoke of "the juggernaut of custom."

38. This contrasts with what happens in *Othello* and *Antony and Cleopatra* where love is presented against a heroic background and where the influence of Marlowe's *Tragedy of Dido* and *Tamburlaine* is visible. See Brian Gibbons, "Unstable Proteus: Marlowe and *Antony and Cleopatra*," in *Shakespeare and Multiplicity* (Cambridge: Cambridge University Press, 1993), 182–202.

JERZY LIMON ON TYBALT'S BEHAVIOR IN THE DUEL

The immediate question is: why does Tybalt run away? He is not a coward, after all. And in any case, what could he be afraid of? It appears to be an uncontrolled reflex act, the motives for which I shall try to establish. It must be something exceptional, seeing that Tybalt—who is very sensitive in matters of honor—resolves on the highly dishonorable act of running away. Was he really horrified by the shameful act of administering that crafty thrust under the arm of Romeo, taking advantage of Mercutio's momentary inattention? But how do we know that the thrust was so treacherous? Hardly anyone noticed it, after all, except Tybalt, who must certainly have felt how deeply the blade penetrated the flesh. Even Mercutio himself appears to be surprised when he confirms laconically, "I am hurt" (91). If Tybalt's guile had been intended by Shakespeare, then the duel would have been played out in such a way that no one would have been left in any doubt. But in fact there is doubt. The whole event takes place unnoticed, seeing that Mercutio has to inform his friends standing close to him (and the spectators in the theater) that he has been wounded. Characteristic, too, is Benvolio's surprise: "What, art thou hurt?" (93), while Romeo takes Mercutio's black humor at its face value and belittles the "scratch": "Courage, man, the hurt cannot be much" (96). The amazement of the witnesses at the whole incident is thus beyond dispute. They are surprised to learn that Mercutio is hurt; they seem not to have noticed themselves.

How, then, do we know that the thrust was administered craftily? We gain this information mainly from the report of

Benvolio when he describes the course of events to the Prince. This report is apparently delivered in the heat of the moment, and yet it is remarkably artful. Seeking to efface the guilt of Mercutio and Romeo, Benvolio lays the blame on Tybalt alone, and in a clearly tendentious manner at that. The inconsistency of Benvolio's statements with the facts has been noticed before, but in this case, scholars have made an exception, unreservedly accepting precisely that part of the description when Benvolio says: "... underneath whose [Romeo's] arm/ An envious thrust from Tybalt hit the life/ Of stout Mercutio ... (169–71). This, then, is a rather detailed description, acting upon the imagination of the hearers, but one cannot help wondering how Benvolio was able to remember such details in view of the fact that previously—that is, during the duel—he did not notice anything and indeed was amazed that anything had happened. Not even Romeo, Mercutio's closest friend, reproaches Tybalt (when the latter returns) with killing Mercutio out of guile. The only person who speaks of "envy" is Benvolio—and this at the moment when, recounting the facts to the Prince, he tries to cleanse Romeo of all blame to show that he had to avenge the death of his treacherously slain friend. Thanks to the particular way in which he presents the course of events, he gains what he intended: the Prince commutes the death sentence to one of banishment. Thus this is not a description that can be relied upon without reservation. Yet this is precisely what happens traditionally in stage management and in critical scholarship.[6] The only exception known to me is Franco Zeffirelli's film version of the play, in which Tybalt's thrust is shown as accidental. In all other productions and in critical interpretations the infamous Tybalt, profiting by a moment of distraction on Mercutio's part, delivers him a treacherous thrust, after which—horrified by his own action—he flees.

Is this really the only way to interpret the flight of Tybalt? We have already reflected on the trustworthiness of Benvolio's words, and in this light it is by no means certain that Tybalt's deed was so disgraceful that he himself was horrified by it. Did he resort to treachery? To answer this question, and at the same time to indicate another possible interpretation, we must return to the moment when Romeo leaps in between the combatants and once again consider the technical particulars of the duel. If we take for granted that Romeo was unarmed, we have a full explanation of his helplessness and irresolution—shown in the fact that instead of jumping to action energetically himself, Romeo first asks Benvolio to act, and then the gentlemen to intervene—resulting from his knowledge of the danger that he would face by leaping unarmed between the combatants. This is why Romeo decides to act only as a last resort—one might say in desperation—when he sees that no one will do it for him. The danger came from the fact that Romeo might run onto the rapier's blade, thereby becoming the unintended victim, one without a weapon and unable to parry a blow.

It seems not improbable that this is what happened: let us imagine that Tybalt strikes in order to hit Mercutio, when suddenly, as if from below the ground, Romeo appears before him. Fortunately Tybalt is an excellent swordsman and always a man of honor: although it is Romeo who was to have been his victim, it was forbidden to even so much as scratch a third person (the one not taking part in the duel), so at the last moment he changes the direction of the thrust (which cannot now simply "hang in the air") and buries the blade into the open space between the trunk and arm of Romeo. And then he feels something that he did not foresee or intend: the blade strikes flesh. It is a mistake to conclude that Tybalt profited by Mercutio's temporary inattention and treacherously dealt him a thrust from under Romeo's arm while he was not looking. That would have been a dishonorable act, inconsistent with binding principles. Mercutio found himself quite by chance in this place that was to be fatal to him; only an unhappy sequence of events causes Tybalt to hit him. The fact that Tybalt's deed was not premeditated or even intimated in advance to anyone is convincingly confirmed for us by the amazement that all the bystanders express. The fortuitousness of Mercutio's death would, moreover, be in harmony with the general character of this early tragedy of Shakespeare, in which chance and misfortune play a dominant role.

Thus when Tybalt, who does not want to injure Romeo, changes the direction of his thrust and strikes the unsuspecting Mercutio, he immediately realizes what has happened. He—almost oversensitive in matters of honor—has committed a shameful act, unworthy of a gentleman. Chance imprints a stain on his honor and that of his family. This is what terrifies him; this is why he loses his head and reacts in a manner that is natural at such times—he runs away. After a time, however, he pulls himself together and, more or less composed, returns, to—well, why does he return? To meet Romeo again? Or perhaps to show that his flight was no more than a weakness of the moment?[7]

(...)

It is not, of course, important whether Benvolio really intended to separate them; what is important is that this intention serves to specify the duration of the duel.[8] This is confirmed, in a sense, by Romeo himself, when he stands as if petrified over the dead Tybalt, as if he could not believe with his own eyes the truth of what had happened. Benvolio urges him: "Romeo, away, be gone! ... Stand not amaz'd" (134–36). Is he astounded at the ease with which he has dispatched his adversary? It seems that only Tybalt's mental state can convincingly explain the fact that such an experienced and skilled swordsman can, in a split second, succumb to a youngster. This mental state, in turn, was provoked by the duel with Mercutio and by its fortuitous and unhappy end.

Notes

6. Among others, Utterback concluded his article with a typical commentary: "Tybalt, the man of precise forms and code of honor, treacherously stabs Mercutio under Romeo's arm" (111). However, in more recent scholarship Benvolio's "strategic" misinterpretation of facts has been noticed; cf., for instance, Joan Ozark Holmer, "'Myself Condemned and Myself Excused': Tragic Effects in *Romeo and Juliet*," *Studies in Philology* 81 (1984): 328–29.

7. Holmer's is a characteristic interpretation of Tybalt's return:

"Amazingly Tybalt now returns to the scene of the crime, still 'furious' (123) and still seeking his original prey. How violent must one be to *return* to kill again, one's sword already bloodily 'neighbor-stained' (1.1.80)? Shakespeare's darker exploration of man's 'rude will' contrasts sharply with Franco Zeffirelli's version of this scene in his well-known film" ("'Myself Condemned,'" 359).

8. The surprising discrepancy between the duration of the duel as suggested by the text and that of theatrical tradition was noticed by Zbierski, *Droga do Werony*, 225.

MARTIN GOLDSTEIN ON THE CAPULET'S ROLE IN THEIR DAUGHTER'S DEATH

I shall suggest in this essay that it is not the feud but a conflict *within* the Capulet household, specifically a disagreement between Capulet and Lady Capulet as to when and whom Juliet is to marry, that is the driving force of the play. The textual evidence for this conflict, though previously overlooked by most commentators, seems compelling, but the reasons why the Capulets disagree and why Capulet changes his mind in the middle of the play are less clear. (...) The resulting reading of *Romeo and Juliet*, casting Old Capulet as a tragic figure to set beside the youthful doomed lovers, can be called a patriarchal version.

(...)

In the first scene, the brawl, started by the servants and exacerbated by Tybalt, leads Capulet and Montague to exchange threats (1, i, 73, 76).[2] These are the last words either will speak in the entire play that show anger at the other house. Note that the symmetrical behavior of the husbands is not shared by the wives. Lady Capulet tells hers:

A crutch, a crutch! Why call you for a sword? (I, i, 74)

while Lady Montague cries out:

Thou shalt not stir one foot to seek a foe. (I, i, 77)

To paraphrase: Lady Montague says, 'I will not let *thee* fight!' while Lady Capulet says, 'You are too old to fight.'

Before this scene is over Montague is asking Benvolio querulously:

Who set this ancient quarrel new abroach? (I, i, 102)

and the next scene, between Capulet and Paris, begins with Capulet's:

'tis not hard I think
For men so old as we to keep the peace. (I, i, 2–3)

We learn quickly that Paris's importunate suit for Juliet's hand is not entirely welcome to Capulet:

My child is yet a stranger in the world,
She hath not seen the change of fourteen years.
Let two more summers wither in their pride
Ere we may think her ripe to be a bride. (I, ii, 7–10)

though Paris's social position and desirability as a suitor require the father to be polite. Paris does not accept Capulet's reason for hesitancy:

Younger than she are happy mothers made. (I, ii, 12)

The old man answers:

And too soon marr'd are those so early made. (I, ii, 13)

and tells Paris that at the feast that night there will be a number of attractive alternatives to Juliet, hardly what one expects a father to say to a desired suitor (I, ii, 24–31).

In the next scene, Lady Capulet goes to Juliet's room to persuade her to marry Paris.

(...)

There are a number of things to be noted in this encounter.

First, Lady Capulet echoes not her husband's view on Juliet's readiness for marriage, but Paris's:

> Younger than you
> Here in Verona, ladies of esteem,
> Are made already mothers. (I, iii, 69–71).

There is clearly a conflict of views between husband and wife regarding Juliet's marriage.[3] Capulet's quotation of the proverb: 'Too soon marr'd ...' suggests further the division between them.[4] Lady Capulet's calling back the Nurse at the beginning of the scene may reflect her feeling that she needs an ally in the household.

(...)

Why does Lady Capulet want Juliet to marry Paris? And why doesn't Old Capulet? We cannot assume his statement to Paris that she is too young is necessarily his real reason: we know that a few days later he will order her to marry him. (...)

Lady Capulet's reason is difficult to discern. It could well be the material and social advantages of a marriage to a wealthy member of the nobility, but it is not obvious why such considerations should lead her to act contrary to her husband's wishes, and surreptitiously. Her urgency calls for a more plausible explanation, but the text fails to provide one. One may speculate that it is a wish to get out of her household a rapidly maturing and attractive daughter, who serves also as an indicator of her own age, but evidence is lacking.

(...)

In Act I, Scene v, we are at the Capulet's ball. Every significant character in the play is present at this scene with the exception of four who should not be there, and one who should. We would not expect the Prince, who would seem to be taking sides in the feud if he came, nor the ascetic Friar Laurence, and of course not the elder Montagues, but where is Paris, who was supposed to woo Juliet in this scene, but doesn't? It would not have slowed the action that much; if Romeo could win Juliet in eighteen lines of dialogue, Paris could have failed in ten. Nor can we assume the wooing took place off-stage, as Juliet informs us when her parents are forcing her to marry Paris:

> I wonder at this haste, that I must wed
> Ere he that should be husband comes to woo. (III, v, 118–119)

(...)

Capulet learns from the furious Tybalt that Romeo is present, and tries to calm him as follows:

> Content thee, gentle coz, let him alone,
> A bears him like a portly gentleman;
> And, to say truth, Verona brags of him
> To be a virtuous and well-governed youth.
> I would not for the wealth of all this town
> Here in my house do him disparagement. (I, v, 64–69)

This is amazingly strong language from Capulet, to whom wealth matters. Tybalt is not appeased, so be old patriarch shows what a temper tantrum he can have when someone who owes him fealty tries to contradict him (I, v, 75–87), apparently going so far as to threaten to cut Tybalt out of his will. This is surely an exaggerated response if Capulet has his heart in the feud and only wants Tybalt to show a cooler judgement about when to pursue it.

(...)

Capulet feels that it is better to endure an unwelcome guest at a party than make a scene. But does not Capulet's good opinion of Romeo say more than this? As the maskers, who to Capulet's knowledge include at least one Montague, are leaving the party, Capulet urges them to stay for 'a trifling foolish banquet' (I, v, 120–121). Is this the customary way to treat unwelcome guests?

A more reasonable reaction to this speech is given in a book by Asimov addressed to a popular rather than a scholarly audience:[9]

Surely the feud is as good as dead when the leader of one side can speak so of the son and heir of the leader of the other side. Capulet speaks so highly of Romeo, in fact, that one could almost imagine that a prospective match between Montague's son and Capulet's daughter would be a capital way of ending the feud.

Let us turn back to the moment when Tybalt realizes that a masked Montague is present; he recognizes the voice as a Montague's (not really plausible, of course), and tells Capulet, who has noticed his perturbation. Capulet's answer is remarkable:

Young Romeo, is it? (I, v, 63)

Without seeing the face or hearing the voice, he knows which Montague it is. He must have had Romeo on his mind, even expecting him to appear at the ball. Why? The hypothesis I offer in answer is as follows: Capulet, grown weary of the feud, and embarrassed by its most recent outbreak, has been thinking of a marriage between his daughter and Romeo as a means of ending it. It is possible, though not necessary, that he expected Romeo to appear at the ball because he knew of the young man's infatuation with his frigid niece Rosaline, one of the guests (I, ii, 74).

(...)

When Romeo has told Friar Laurence of his new love, the Friar, like Capulet, sees a marriage between Romeo and Juliet as a means of ending the feud (II, iv, 87–88), and performs the clandestine wedding happily; presumably he means to call

Montague and Capulet together to inform them of it after the marriage has been consummated. However, before either he or Capulet can make whatever moves they have been contemplating, events take matters out of their control: Romeo has slain Tybalt, the citizens of Verona are outraged at the renewed feud.

(...)

The Prince's next words decree the banishment of Romeo:

> And for that offence
> Immediately do we exile him hence ...
> I will be deaf to pleading and excuses;
> Nor tears nor prayers shall purchase out abuses.
> Therefore use none. Let Romeo hence in hasten
> Else when he is found, that hour is his last. (III, i, 188–189,
> 194–196)

Though the words are harsh the decision is a lenient one, as is clearly recognized by Friar Laurence, who in (III, iii) tells the depressed Romeo three times how fortunate he is, first describing the Prince's 'doom' as 'a gentler judgement' (line 10), then saying:

> the kind Prince,
> Taking thy part, has rush'd aside the law
> And turn'd that black word 'death' to banishment.
> This is dear mercy and thou seest it not. (III, iii, 25–28)

and later:

> The law that threaten'd death becomes thy friend
> And turns it to exile. There art thou happy. (III, iii, 139–140)

Could the Prince so easily have passed this judgement unless Capulet's silence was seen by him as assent?

But that same silence must also have widened the division

between Capulet and his Lady into a breach, indeed a breach between him and her side of the family. Evidence for that breach is provided in (III, v), when Lady Capulet tells Juliet of her plan to poison the banished Romeo:

I'll send to one in Mantua,
Where that same banish'd runagate doth live,
Shall give him such an unaccustom'd dram
That he shall soon keep Tybalt company ... (III, v, 88–91)

'I'll send', not 'We'll send'. Note that she is the only member of the older generation who expresses the eye-for-an-eye ethic of a feud.

(...)

We arrive at the final scene at the Capulet family tomb, the full significance of which, in particular the lengthy summary by Friar Laurence of what is already known to the audience and which has troubled many critics, has been clarified in a remarkable essay by Bertrand Evans.[12] Evans interprets the play, in accord with its prologue, as a tragedy of Fate, but in which the manner in which Fate operates is made specific:

Romeo and Juliet is a tragedy of unawareness. Fate ... working out its purposes without either a human villain or a supernatural agent ... operates through the common condition of not knowing. Participants in the action ... contribute one by one the indispensable stitches which make the pattern, and contribute them without knowing; that is to say, they act when they do not know the truth of the situation in which they act.

The unawareness includes not only the obvious unawareness of everyone except Friar Laurence of the love between Romeo and Juliet, but an unawareness on the part of each and every character (including Friar Laurence) that at each moment of decisive action leads to an intensification of the rush towards doom. Examples given by Evans include the unawareness of Capulet's illiterate servant in Act I, scene ii that it is Romeo Montague whose help he asks, the initial unawareness of both Romeo and Juliet that the person each is attracted to at the ball is a member of the enemy family (I, v), the unawareness of both Tybalt and Mercutio of the clandestine marriage (III, i), Capulet's unawareness of the real reason for Juliet's submission in IV, ii, Paris's unawareness of Romeo's reason for being at the tomb (V, iii), and of special significance, Friar Laurence's unawareness that Romeo's servant Balthasar has informed his master of Juliet's apparent death, an unawareness that causes the Friar to arrive at the tomb too late to prevent Romeo's suicide.

In the scene between the tearful Juliet and her angry father, the unawareness of each of the thoughts and situation of the other are farther indispensable stitches. Capulet is of course unaware of Juliet's marriage; Juliet in turn is unaware of her father's hope for a reconciling marriage with Romeo and unaware, as is Capulet also, of the divided state of mind that fuels his fury.

Hear me with patience but to speak a word. (III, v, 159)

she begs, but she is cowed by that fury, and the word is unspoken.

In the end, the clouds of unawareness are lifted when Friar Laurence, Balthasar, and Paris's page tell their stories. Does Capulet recognize the irony that the marriage he once hoped would end the feud has, in fact, ended it? Even so, he is still man enough to speak first:

O brother Montague, give me thy hand. (V, iii, 295)

and to make his sad little joke:

This is my daughter's jointure, for no more
Can I demand. (V, iii, 296–297)

After this, who needs those gilded statues?

Notes

2. Text references are to *The Arden Edition of the Works of William Shakespeare: Romeo and Juliet*. Brian Gibbons, Editor. London, 1980.

3. Noted by Alfred Harbage in *Shakespeare: A Reader's Guide*, New York, 1963.

4. In the Zeffirelli film (*Romeo and Juliet*, Paramount, 1968, Franco Zeffirelli, Director), Capulet, as he says these words, glances at his wife, who is in view but is not a party to his conversation with Paris.

9. Isaac Asimov, *Asimov's Guide to Shakespeare*, New York, 1993, page 485.

12. Bertrand Evans, 'The Brevity of Friar Laurence', *Publications of the Modern Language Association*, Vol. 65, No. 2, March, 1950, pp. 841–865.

JOSEPH A. PORTER ON MERCUTIO'S SPEECH AND SPACE

As Mercutio crosses the threshold from Brooke into Shakespeare he acquires not only a brother, a friendship, and a death but also a distinctively eloquent and vividly characteristic voice. To the extent that he stands outside the main plot, neither affecting it nor being affected by it until his death, mere language has a particular prominence with him. As is well known, Mercutio is a landmark in Shakespeare's early development of characterisation in distinctive speech, and much of the impressionistic admiration (as well as some of the disapproval) he has elicited has been for his speech.

(...)

The theory and study of speech acts has come to be called pragmatics, the term formed in parallel with the traditional levels of linguistic analysis, phonetics, syntactics, and semantics.

(...)

The 'pragmatic space' in which speech acts exist has for its

106

dimensions the distinguishing features of the acts.[11] This space may be conceived of as absolute and Newtonian, but for a literary text, and especially for a play, it seems more reasonable to posit a relativistic space, one determined and successively modified by the speech acts it contains.

(...)

Mercutio's speech acts, then, constitute a characteristic manifold in significant contrast with that constituted by the speech acts of such other characters as Romeo and Benvolio, and full of resonances with Shakespeare's received Mercury.

(...)

After Mercutio's last exit assisted by Benvolio Romeo speaks immediately of him in soliloquy, giving him the first three of the series of encomiums in obsequy that extends through the remainder of the scene:

> This gentleman, the Prince's near ally,
> My very friend, hath got this mortal hurt
> In my behalf.
> (III.i.111–13)

So begins what may be called Mercutio's exit limen, or threshold; that is, the space between his last appearance onstage and the last direct references to him in the play, at V.iii.75.[36] It answers his entrance limen, the space between the first reference to him, when he is named with his brother Valentine in the guest list at I.ii.68, and his first appearance onstage at I.iv.S.D., but it contains almost the entire second half of the play, with several important references to him beginning with this one, as well as other sorts of echo. Indeed as an exit limen for so important a character Mercutio's seems unprecedented in Shakespeare.

(...)

This amplification keeps Mercutio very much present in the mind of the audience through the eighty-eight lines of the scene that follow his final exit, and so prepares for his continuing subliminal presence through most of the rest of the play. When Romeo in the Capulet tomb identifies the man he has killed as 'Mercutio's kinsman' (V.iii.75), the reference seems not gratuitous; rather it comes with a kind of naturalness or even inevitability, invoking a presence already immanent among the present and imminent corpses, a presence reactivated seven lines before by the 'conjuration'.

That presence is immanent because we miss Mercutio; we want him in the final scene, more perhaps than we want the actually present and named Paris and Tybalt, more than we want the other major absent characters, Benvolio and the Nurse (whose absence goes unmarked by any reference to either of them and may go unremarked by an audience), and certainly more than we want Lady Montague, the only other absent character referred to.[38] The explicit references just discussed have kept the absent Mercutio present in our minds, and so have other sorts of echo, such as the phonetic echo in the line with which the Prince closes Mercutio's death scene, 'Mercy but murders' (l. 99). And we may see a trace of Mercutio in IV.ii. When Capulet begins the scene by handing a guest list to a servant with the command 'So many guests invite as here are writ' (IV.ii.1) he enacts a reprise of Mercutio's introduction into the play. Moments later Mercutio's shadow falls over Capulet's impulsive and disastrous decision to advance the marriage day from Thursday to Wednesday— *mercredi*, Mercury's day.

The aubade of *Romeo and Juliet*, III.v, provides a good example of Mercutio's immanence. Juliet's claim that the daylight is a meteor exhaled by the sun to be a torchbearer (l. 14) recalls not only the wind and breath associated with Mercutio but also Romeo's denial of his friend's request, 'Give me a torch, I am not for this ambling' (I.iv.11). Mercutio also inheres in traces of the god Mercury who seems almost to hover over the scene, to effect the lovers' separation in one of the god's own liminal hours, the dawn, and to send the hero on the road. Traces of Mercury are associated with the lark and with the daylight. The lark is 'herald' (l. 6) and it sings 'harsh discords' (l. 28) with an echo of the words of Mercury at the end of *Love's Labour's Lost*, and the image of the severing clouds and day 'tiptoe on the misty mountain tops' (l. 10) echoes Mercury's skimming the clouds and pausing on Mt Atlas, as in *Aeneid* 4.

In addition to his posthumous presence in traces like these, Mercutio is immanent through his exit limen because his death occurs offstage. Any number of factors may have been involved in Shakespeare's decision to remove Mercutio's death from our view. It gives Romeo a moment alone onstage (except for servants) to deliver the soliloquy expressing his dawning awareness of the gravity of the situation. And then possibly the actor playing Mercutio needed to exit so that he could change and re-enter thirty-two lines and a swordfight later as the prince, in which case, by Meagher's principles of economy and recognition reference to Mercutio would inhere in everything the Prince does and says, including the last words of the play.[39]

Whatever its other effects, Mercutio's offstage death fixes Mercutio in a boundary region between life and death, or elevates him above that boundary. In all fictions including 'reality' the more attractive a person the more likely we are somewhere in our minds to treat reports of his or her death as greatly exaggerated.

(...)

In Mercutio's onstage presence too, before he crosses the mortal boundary into his long exit threshold, he embodies the liminality of the Mercury who presides over the wild border regions, the bean who stands by the roadside to guide a wayfarer or a *romeo*. Boundaries—that of the ancient feud, those of gender and generation, those between night and day and life and death—crisscross Mercutio's play, and much of its action transpires at such Mercurially liminal times and sites as dawn, the city walls, the garden and balcony, the interurban road, and the entrance to the tomb. Above all others Mercutio before his death manifests this liminality in his behaviour, as when he turns aside from his companions as if rapt in his talk of dreams, fantasy, and the wind that, in Benvolio's words, 'blows us from ourselves' (I.v.104).

Mercutio's social structures are themselves textbook examples of the liminal as expounded by Van Gennep, Turner, and others.[42] As with that stage in rites of passage and initiations when the initiates have left behind old social affiliations, and perhaps names, without yet having assumed new ones, so that they live together for a time outside the ordinary dwelling area, in radical equality and strong bondedness, so with the trio of Benvolio, Romeo, and Mercutio.

The avatar of this world is Mercutio. He summons Romeo back to it with his conjuration, and he works to hold both his friends in it with the verbal play he initiates and leads with both of them, and with his scorn of the love that ends in marriage and, in the Queen Mab speech, of adult occupations. But Mercutio's eloquence is for nought: Benvolio slips away, Romeo falls in love and marries, and the mortally wounded Mercutio is left to curse. As the form of his curse shows, a subtext of his concluding situation, at least in his understanding, is an *in trivio* Mercury without any *romei* to direct. They have all retreated to the shelter of their houses, which he curses for being houses. And since the Montagues and Capulets stand opposed, and since their opposition (combined with an individual attraction across the hostile boundary) is the cause of Mercutio's death, he has in a sense at last traded places with Romeo in the triad with Juliet. Now standing between them, Mercutio curses them and their houses because he is destroyed by them. Thus in Mercutio's final tragic configuration the liminal has become central, the god of the wild border region has become god of the agora.

Notes

11. Geoffrey N. Leech, *Explorations in Semantics and Pragmatics* (Amsterdam, 1980), p. 114.

36. A general dramaturgic theory of characters' limens or thresholds could be useful. It would need to take into account not only cases like Mercutio's, where reference to the character precedes his first entrance and follows his last exit, but also cases with no entrance or exit limen, where no reference precedes or follows the character's appearance onstage, and perhaps—though this raises problems—negative limens. The theory might take into account a given limens comparative fullness (or emptiness) of reference to the character. Mercutio's exit limen, for instance, especially in its beginning, seems comparatively full of reference to him. The theory could also be made to handle interliminal or subliminal spaces between a given character's onstage appearances.

38. According to John C. Meagher in 'Economy and Recognition: Thirteen Shakespearean Puzzles', *Shakespeare Quarterly*, 35 (1984), 7–21, Lady Montague and the Nurse must both be absent in the final scene because their actors are present in other roles. Meagher bases his theory on the seemingly required doubling of roles imposed on Shakespeare by the size of his troupe, and on what he takes to be Shakespeare's exploitation of that limitation in his metatheatric use of the audience's presumed recognition of actors playing doubled roles. Because Lady Montague's absence creates too obvious an asymmetry to be ignored, Shakespeare has Montague announce her death on the spot 'rather lamely' (p. 12). But 'one abrupt demise is enough; having eliminated Lady Montague explicitly, it would not be diplomatic for Shakespeare to try to get by with killing the Nurse through an analogous grief' (p. 12). Meagher holds that we in fact do miss the Nurse in the final scene. And see note 39 below. In Q I, incidentally, Benvolio is mentioned in V.iii.36.

39. Meagher, ibid., p. 13, has Mercutio doubled with Paris, but other arrangements are feasible. Mercutio's doubling with the prince would 'explain' the peculiar offstage death. Booth offers no more compelling reason for it. But Mercutio's exit to die offstage followed shortly by the Prince's entrance does suggest that the roles of Mercutio and the Prince might have been doubled, or perhaps 'tripled', since he asks us also to entertain the possibility that the same actor might have played Paris, an admitted improbability given the necessary legerdemain with Paris's body in Act V scene iii to permit the Prince's entrance in rile same scene. While the proposed tripling would provide a pleasing reflection of the kinship of the three characters, Stephen Booth in *'King Lear'*, *'Macbeth'*, *Indefinition, and Tragedy* (New Haven, CT, 1983) offers no more compelling reason for it. But Mercutio's exit to die offstage followed shortly by the Prince's entrance looks more like an accommodation to doubling than anything else in the play.

42. See Arnold Van Gennep, *The Rites of Passage* (1901, trans. Monika B. Vizedom and Gabrielle L. Caffe [Chicago, 1960]) for the three stages of rites of passage (i.e., separation, margin or limen, and reaggregation) and Turner, 'Betwixt' and *Ritual*, for an expansion of liminality to a border region incorporating some of Van Gennep's stage of separation, and for the liminal society: 'The liminal group is a community or comity of comrades' ('Betwixt', p. 100). David Bevington, *Action is Eloquence: Shakespeare's Language of Gesture* (Cambridge, MA, 1984) uses Turner notably: Victor Witter Turner, 'Betwixt and Between: The Liminal Period', in *Rites de Passage* (1964, repr. ch. 4 in *The Forest of Symbols: Aspects of Ndembu Ritual* [Ithaca, NY, 1967] and *The Ritual Process: Structure and Anti-Structure* (Chicago, 1969).

JILL L. LEVENSON ON SHAKESPEARE AND ADOLESCENCE

Love, Death, and Adolescence. One source of affect in *Romeo and Juliet* must be the mythical component of the narrative, potential which the dramatic version exploits to a far greater degree than the novellas. Again and again Shakespeare reinforces *Liebestod* and resonant myths, not only with references to Cupid and Venus but with allusions to unrelated Ovidian stories connecting disaster and transformation: Phaëton, the most prominent (2.2.4, 2.4.9, 3.2.1–4, 5.3.306), as well as Danaë (1.1.210), Echo (2.1.207–9), Julius Caesar (3.2.22–5), Philomel (3.5.4), and Proserpina (5.3.105). At times citations of supporting myth and legend appear in unlikely places, such as Mercutio's catalogue of five tragic heroines in his mockery of Romeo as lover (2.3.40–2). Despite comic distractions like this, promises of woe to come occur everywhere in the play. The motif of death as Juliet's bridegroom, identified by M.M. Mahood and T.J.B. Spencer,[1] is introduced at the end of the fourth scene (ll. 247–8) and repeated until its enactment in 5.3. Wordplay and irony also anticipate the tragic close. On seeing Juliet at the dance, Romeo observes 'Beauty too rich for use, for earth too dear' (see 1.4.160 n.). In their first private conversation Juliet confesses, as she compares Romeo to a pet bird, 'Yet I should kill thee with much cherishing' (2.1.229). The familiar version of the wedding scene concentrates foreboding in the exchange between Friar Laurence and Romeo (2. 5.1–15).[2]

The play (...) enhances the rite of passage which the myth represents. While the novellas emphasize the lovers' failure to make the social transition symbolized by marriage, they present little psychological complexity. Literary conventions which stylize thought and emotion allow the protagonists almost no individuality: Romeo and Juliet are patterns of young love, his age unspecified, hers noted (daring her father's marriage negotiations) as sixteen in Brooke, eighteen or so in the others. By contrast, the dramatic version catches the lovers specifically in the early and middle phases of adolescence. Its portrayal off these phases, remarkable for its accuracy and thoroughness, is animated by sexual energy. When wordplay imitates sexual play, it expresses thoughts and sensations typical of this often chaotic period of transition.[3] The staging itself, readily adaptable to film, charges events:

> Visually, the play remains memorable for a number of reported images—street brawls, swords flashing to the hand, torches rushing on and off, crowds gathering. The upper stage is used frequently, with many opportunities for leaping or scrambling or stretching up and down and much play between upper and lower areas. The dominant feelings we get as an audience are oppressive heat, sexual desire, a frequent whiz-bang exhilarating kinesthesia of speed and clash, and above all a feeling of the keeping-down and separation of highly charged bodies, whose pressure toward release and whose sudden discharge determine the rhythm of the play.[4]

(...)

In its portrayal of adolescent phases, *Romeo and Juliet* uses the sequence of the well-known story as a point of departure. It adds scenes and shorter passages to the fictional narrative which enlarge the social worlds of the lovers before reducing them, and which therefore complicate relationships with families or friends. Consequently the changes of adolescence, part of a larger dynamic, set off repercussions at every level of the action: the protagonists verbalize them and act them out; Romeo's friends mirror or disagree with his behaviour; and the older generation, misconstruing almost all of the signs, hasten events towards calamity.

(...)

In effect, the play simulates what Anna Freud calls 'the atmosphere in which the adolescent lives':

> ... [the] anxieties, the height of elation or depth of despair, the quickly rising enthusiasms, the utter hopelessness, the burning—or at other times sterile—intellectual and philosophical preoccupations, the yearning for freedom, the sense of loneliness, the feeling of oppression by the parents, the impotent rages or active hates directed against the adult world, the erotic crushes—whether homosexually or heterosexually directed—the suicidal fantasies, etc.[5]

Although writers since antiquity had recognized and recorded the experience of adolescence, none had dramatized it so comprehensively.[6]

The play observes the transitional phase from an adult's point of view as the younger generation assume the attitudes typical of the process; it also adopts the adolescent's point of view as the developing personality responds to family and other social values and beliefs. Consequently it presents adolescence in Verona not only as it is perceived by those who have survived it, usually in a distant or vanished past, but, also as it is felt by those who are growing through it until violence abruptly stops their progress. Finally the play totalizes this experience, which psychoanalytic theory and recent data continue to link with emotional turmoil: the whole adolescent population, including the most stable personalities, feel the pressures of new sexual impulses and socialization as adults.[7] The dramatic action displays a range of adolescent behaviours from Benvolio to Tybalt, less disturbed to more disturbed, showing these figures in relation to one another and to adults—especially father-figures.[8]

(...)

Clearly Shakespeare's additions and adjustments contribute to the narrative's inclusiveness as well as its various ironies. One modern study of adolescence begins with *Romeo and Juliet* 2.2, the exchange between Romeo and Friar Laurence about Romeo's inconstancy. Original to the play, this dialogue sets adolescent intensity and impatience against adult perplexity and rationalization; its tension is diverted rather than resolved. Friar Laurence may joke about Romeo's passions—tears, sighs, and groans over changing objects of love—but, he never acknowledges their sources, and at last he will indulge them in an attempt to end the feud (ll. 90–92).[9] Through the rest of the play this pattern continues: Friar Laurence redirects not only Juliet's suicidal inclinations (4.1), as his prototypes had, but also Romeo's (3.3), both efforts to reconcile the families. In a few days the repressed feelings overwhelm both the protagonists and Friar Laurence. They also overwhelm the other adults in the play, from Montague to the Nurse, who misunderstand the younger generation in their charge. Again and again the drama focuses on this kind of misunderstanding which is probably, in Peter Blos's summation, 'as old as generations themselves'.[10] The lovers and parent-figures never confront their growing distance from one another; and the parent-figures, from one angle, represent adults in adolescent fantasy and perception.[11]

The peer group which centres on Mercutio, the leader of high social status who takes the greatest risks, represents a constant of adolescent experience observed by Aristotle in his *Rhetoric*: '[Young men] are fonder of their friends, intimates, and companions than older men are, because they like spending their days in the company of others'.[12] In Western cultures the male peer group provides space for transition from childhood dependencies to adult relationships: the adolescent experiments with social conventions—dress, gesture, vocabulary—as he establishes his sexual identity according to the group's standard; he may also experiment with fantasy and introspection.[13] Nevertheless, the family remains a source of shelter and security: Romeo, still a ward, will follow Mercutio and Benvolio to dinner at his father's house (2.3.130–2).[14]

Like the signs of dissonance between generations, those of interaction within the peer group are obvious in the play. From the approach to Capulet's party, the three named members show concern with style and decorum, sometimes pointedly dismissing what others think. When Romeo asks if they will enter with a formal speech, for example, Benvolio responds, 'the date is out of such prolixity', and he concludes:

But let them measure us by what they will,
We'll measure them a measure and be gone.
(1.4.3–8)

Mercutio, putting on a mask required by the occasion, asks, 'What care I | What curious eye doth quote deformities?' (ll. 28–9). Since they plan to present themselves in a uniform way, Mercutio attempts to talk Romeo out of the loverlike attitude that sets him apart. His idiom of choice is the pun, unsubtle and ribald, characteristic of the language these young men share. Although not unique to them—Samson and Gregory introduce bawdy wordplay as contest when the play opens—the pun combines with other rhetorical figures to produce a distinct mode of expression, what Erik Homburger Erikson would call a 'strange code'.[15]

(...)

Romeo and Juliet meet in this incoherent world of shifting identities and relationships, each at a different phase of adolescent development. According to 1.2 and 1.3, Juliet has

116

just entered adolescence from latency, its juncture with childhood. When she first appears she reveals no consciousness of her sexuality, behaviour characteristic of girls her age, despite the subject of the conversation: 'How stands your dispositions to be married?' (1.3.67). 'It is an honour that I dream not of' (1. 68), Juliet responds, and she is just as abstract: when her mother asks, 'can you like of Paris' love?' (I. 98):

> I'll look to like, if looking liking move.
> But no more deep will I indart mine eye
> Than your consent gives strength to make it fly.
> (ll. 99–101)

At this point Juliet accommodates herself to social conventions which take no account of the transitional period she has begun: her mother and nurse expect the child to turn into a woman without delay.[16]

By comparison Romeo has advanced farther, both in becoming autonomous and in directing his sexual feelings towards an object. Shakespeare makes this object Rosaline, a Capulet, identifying the anonymous lady of the sources with the enemy house. As a result Romeo's first love anticipates his second, and both externalize the emotional conflict which he attempts to articulate in formal, poetic terms, they represent not only unattainable but forbidden desire, sexual impulses which may revive his earliest, Oedipal sensations.[17] In isolation or company Romeo seeks the 'sharp, intense affective states' which compensate for the losses of adolescence, especially detachment from parental figures.[18] He uses Petrarchan language to describe the anxiety of a self-conscious personality loosed from its moorings: 'Tut, I have lost myself, I am not here; | This is not Romeo, he's some other where' (see 1.1.193–4 n. and 'Tragedy, Comedy, Sonnet' below).

Notes

1. Mahood, p. 57, and Spencer's edition, 1.5.135 n.
2. The impression of imminent disaster is less intense in the 1597

version of *Romeo and Juliet*, which has fewer lines to anticipate its ending and different wedding scene. (see below, 'The Mobile Text'.)

3. On the eroticism of verbal wit, see Stephen Greenblatt, 'Fiction and Friction', in *Reconstructing Individualism*, pp. 48–50.

4. Michael Goldman, *Shakespeare and the Energies of Drama* (Princeton, 1972), p. 33.

5. 'Adolescence', *Psychoanalytic Study of the Child*, 13 (1958), 260.

6. Often writers describe this stage as part of their own inner landscapes. Norman Kiell cites a variety of early examples throughout *The Universal Experience of Adolescence* (New York, 1964). At the beginning of *The Adolescent Passage: Developmental Issues* (New York, 1979), Peter Blos quotes a passage from Aristotle's *Rhetoric* which gives a circumstantial account of male adolescence (pp. 12–13). On ideas characteristic of Shakespeare's period, see Ilana Krausman Ben-Amos, *Adolescence and Youth in Early Modern England* (New Haven and London, 1994), especially Chapters 1 and 8.

7. See, for example, Harvey Golombek and Peter Morton, 'Adolescents over Time: A Longitudinal Study of Personality Development', *Adolescent Psychiatry*, 18 (1992), 213–84.

8. On Tybalt see, for instance, 1.4.202–3 n. Two essays regard Tybalt as a troubled adolescent who compensates for his insecure masculinity with hostile aggressiveness: Marjorie Kolb Cox, 'Adolescent Processes in *Romeo and Juliet*', *Psychoanalytic Review*, 63 (1976), 386, and Sara Munson Deats, 'The Conspiracy of Silence in Shakespeare's Verona: *Romeo and Juliet*', in *Youth Suicide Prevention: Lessons from Literature*, ed. Deats and Lagretta Tallent Lenker (New York and London, 1989), p. 81.

9. Henry P. Coppolillo, 'The Tides of Change in Adolescence', in *The Course of Life*, vol. 4: *Adolescence*, ed. Stanley I. Greenspan and George H. Pollock (Madison, Conn., 1991), pp. 235–6.

10. *Adolescent Passage*, p. 14.

11. See Hyman L. Muslin, 'Romeo and Juliet: The Tragic Self in Adolescence', *Adolescent Psychiatry*, 10 (1982), 142, and Katherine Dalsimer, *Female Adolescence: Psychoanalytic Reflections on Works of Literature* (New Haven and London, 1986), p. 81. Dalsimer adds that the match with Paris is the same type of representation.

12. Quoted in Blos, *Adolescent Passage*, p. 13.

13. Both Blos, *Adolescent Passage*, and Kiell, *Universal Experience*, devote chapters to the subject of peer groups. See also Erik Homburger Erikson, 'The Problem of Ego Identity', *Journal of the American Psychoanalytic Association*, 4 (1956), 72–3.

14. On Romeo's status see Bruce W. Young, 'Haste, Consent, and

Age at Marriage: Some Implications of Social History for *Romeo and Juliet*', *Iowa State Journal of Research* 62 (1988), 465.

15. 'Ego Identity', 73.

16. Both Cox, 'Adolescent Processes', 383–4, and Dalsimer, *Female Adolescence*, pp. 84–90, discuss the psychological implications of this scene.

17. See Cox, 'Adolescent Processes', 381, and Dalsimer, *Female Adolescence*, p. 93.

18. Blos, *Adolescent Passage*, p. 159, defines these states.

BARBARA EVERETT ON
THE NURSE'S REMINISCENCES

The heroine of *Romeo and Juliet* enters the play late. Not until the third scene of the first Act is she called on-stage by her mother and her Nurse, who are also appearing here for the first time. The latter part of this scene is given to Lady Capulet's brisk and formal announcement of an offer for her daughter, with Juliet's timid and obedient response. All the earlier part of it is dominated by the Nurse, and her reminiscences of the past set the tone for the first appearance of the only three really important women in this romantic and domestic tragedy. Lady Capulet's conventional niceties make their point too, but it is the Nurse who holds the stage.

(...)

[T]he major function of the Nurse's speech is to provide a *natural* context for the motif of 'death-marked love' which governs the play. Such intimations of mortality as occur here hardly rise to tragic dignity. But it is commonly agreed that *Romeo and Juliet* makes tragedy out of the lyrical and comical. The Nurse's jokes operate well within that region of the 'painfully funny' which comes fully and deeply into being at the death of Mercutio. Indeed, one might call Mercutio's death-scene, with the astonishing death-blow given unheralded to the irresponsibly free and funny voting man, a perfect match or counter-poise in a harsh vein to what is set forth here with a rough tenderness. What the Nurse says at this early point acts as a semi-choric commentary, helping to build up the background of suggestions which in the earlier part of the play act as am unconscious persuasion stronger than the explicit feud-motif in accounting for the catastrophe. It might be objected that this would demand an audience impossibly acute, able at once to laugh at the Nurse, relish her 'character', and respond to the more impersonal connotations of what she says. But it must be pointed out that for the original theatre audience this charmingly comical account of a marriageable girl's infancy was narrated on a stage hung everywhere with black. The reference to 'Juliet and her Romeo' at the end of the play certainly makes it sound a story already very familiar, almost fabulous; but even those not familiar with the tale could hardly fail to observe that a death was likely at some point to take place: that they were assisting at a tragedy. They could not be wholly unprepared to hear, at the very least, a touch of painful irony in the lines that close the Nurse's affectionate apostrophe:

Thou was the prettiest babe that e're I nursed;
An I might live to see thee married once,
I have my wish.

'Married once' just about covers Juliet's case. It seems worth while to look at the Nurse's speech in rather closer focus than it has received.

The passage falls into three sections: the first concerned with Juliet's age and birthday ('On Lammas Eve at night shall she be fourteen'), the second with the child's weaning, and the third with the child's fall. First things first: the birthday. Lammas Eve is July 31st, and so an appropriate date (as the New Penguin editor has pointed out) for a heroine named from July. But there may be a particular resonance in the festival date, which is thrice repeated, with all effect as much of ritual as of wandering memory. The Christian feast of Lammas took the place of what was possibly the most important of the four great pagan festival days, the midsummer feast. 'Laminas' itself meant originally 'loaf-mass', the sacrament at which were offered loaves made from the first ripe corn, the first fruits of the harvest. One therefore might expect Lammas Eve to carry, for an Elizabethan consciousness, mixed and fugitive but none the less suggestive associations, both with Midsummer Eve and with harvest festival. Such associations would be appropriate. For *Romeo and Juliet* is a summer tragedy as its companion-piece, *A Midsummer Night's Dream*, is a summer comedy.

(...)

A reference to Lammas, then, may carry a Proleptic suggestion both of the fall that follows the midsummer equinox in the course of nature and of the sacrificial offerings of first-fruits. And there is a further point to be made, concerning Elizabethan idiom. The expression 'latter Lammas' was used to mean 'Never'—a time that will never come. The more sombre, if tender side of these hints is strengthened by the Nurse's references to Juliet's dead foster-sister, Susan.

(...)

The first of the two incidents she recalls concerns Juliet's weaning; which we may now call, in view of that movement to maturity involved with the whole tragic action, Juliet's first weaning. The interesting fact about the earthquake that ushers in this first movement of the narrative is not (or not only) that several such actually happened in England in the last decades of the sixteenth century, but that in this speech one happens at the same time as the weaning. This particular specimen is a poetic and not a historical event and it takes place within a context of its own. On the one hand there is the earthquake, a natural cataclysm of extraordinary magnitude, such as people remember and talk about and date things by: something quite beyond the personal—really unstoppable: it shook the dovehouse. On the other hand, there is the dovehouse, symbol—as Shakespeare's other references to doves reveal—of mildness and peace and affectionate love; and there is the Nurse, 'Sitting in the sun under the dove-house wall'; and in the middle of this sun and shelter, framed as in some piece of very early genre painting, there is the weaning of the child. The most domestic and trivial event, personal and simply human as it is, is set beside the violently alien and impersonal earthquake, the two things relating only as they co-exist in a natural span (or as recalled by the wandering mind of a natural); and because they relate, they interpenetrate. The Nurse's 'confused' thought-processes contemplate the earthquake with that curious upside-downness that is merely the reflex of those who communicate most with very small children and who speak as though they saw things as small children see them. Her 'Shake, quoth the dove-house' has not been quite helpfully enough glossed, presumably because few Shakespeare editors are sufficiently acquainted with what might be said to a very small child about an earthquake. It does not simply mean, as has been suggested, 'the dovehouse shook'; it allows the unfluttered dovecote to satirise the earthquake, as in a comical baby mock-heroic—to be aloof and detached from what is happening to it. Thus, if the dovecote gains a rational upper hand and superior tone over the earthquake, the same kind of reversal occurs in that the weaning produces an (if anything) even more formidable storm in the small child, a cataclysmic infant rage satirised by the unfluttered Nurse:

> To see it tetchy, and fall out with the dug!
> Shake, quoth the dove-house. 'Twas no need, I trow,
> To hid me trudge.

(...)

The account of the weaning is less 'muddled' than so designed as to give the Nurse impressive associations such as recur much later and in the far more famous image, 'the beggar's nurse, and Caesar's'. The Nurse, lively and deathly as she is, with 'wormwood to lily dug', is Juliet's natural context, the place she starts from (and Capulet's pun is relevant here: 'Earth hath swallowed all my hopes but she; She is the hopeful lady of my earth'). Bidding the Nurse 'trudge' is the effort, one might say, of the horizontal man to be a vertical one—the human move to surpass the mere milieu of things.

The Nurse's second anecdote adds a brief, ludicrous, but none the less shrewd comment on that hunger for verticality, the perils of standing 'high-lone'. The ironic and pathetic notes of the earlier part of the speech modulate here into something brisk and broadly comic; hence the introduction of the 'merry man', the Nurse's husband, as chief actor—a replacement of surrogate mother by surrogate father, which explains the slight fore-echoes of the relationship of Yorick and the Gravedigger with Hamlet. Yet even here there is more than the merely anecdotal. The iterations, like those in the first part of the speech, are not circumscribed by the effect of the tedium of folly; there are echoes of the wisdom of folly too.

'Thou wilt fall backward when thou has more wit,
Wilt thou not, Jule?' And, by my holidam,
The pretty wretch left crying, and said 'Ay'.
 'Wilt thou not, Jule?' quoth he;
And, pretty fool, it stinted, and said 'Ay'.
'Wilt thou not, Jule?' It stinted, and said 'Ay'.

Such iterations are as close to the rhythm of ritual as they are to tedium. And they are a reminder of the presence in this play of what Yeats called 'custom and ceremony', of the ordered repetitions that frame the life of generations:

Now, by my maidenhead at twelve year old ...
I was your mother much upon these years
That you are now a maid ...
 I have seen the day
That I have worn a visor and could tell
A whispering tale in a fair lady's ear ...

Now old desire doth in his death-bed lie,
And young affection gapes to he his heir ...

This feeling for age-old process is perhaps caught up into a casual phrase of the Nurse's, a warm appreciation of the old man's unsubtle joke:

I warrant, an I should live a thousand years,
I never should forget it.

Involved with the husband's repetitions, one might say, is the rhythm of an existence unchanged in a thousand years. Under Juliet's particular gift, in the action that follows, for saying 'Ay' to a situation, lies any small child's easily observed habit of hopefully saying, 'Yes' to anything; and under that—so the Nurse's speech suggests—lies a resilience and resurgence in nature itself.

All in all, there is considerable density of reference in the Nurse's speech. And this density is not in itself affected by the explanation we find for it: whether we choose to talk of a tissue of inexplicit conceptions within the mind of the artist himself, or whether we like to think of it as some more conscious artistry that expects a more conscious response, does not matter. The degree of deliberation that ever exists on Shakespeare's part does not seem a fruitful critical issue: it contains too many questions impossible to answer. What one can say is that the Nurse's speech presents an image of Juliet's past that happens to contain, or that contains with a purpose, a premonitory comment on her future.

Works by William Shakespeare*

Henry VI, part 1, circa 1589–1592.

Henry VI, part 2, circa 1590–1592.

Henry VI, part 3, circa 1590–1592.

Richard III, circa 1591–1592.

The Comedy of Errors, circa 1592–1594.

Venus and Adonis, 1593.

Titus Andronicus, 1594.

The Taming of the Shrew, 1594.

The Two Gentlemen of Verona, 1594.

The Rape of Lucrece, 1594.

Love's Labor's Lost, circa 1594–1595.

Sir Thomas More, circa 1594–1595.

King John, circa 1594–1596.

Richard II, circa 1595.

Romeo and Juliet, circa 1595–1596.

A Midsummer Night's Dream, circa 1595–1596.

The Merchant of Venice, circa 1596–1597.

Henry IV, part 1, circa 1596–1597.

Henry IV, part 2, circa 1597.

The Merry Wives of Windsor, 1597.

Much Ado About Nothing, circa 1598–99.

The Passionate Pilgrim, 1599.

Henry V, 1599.

Julius Caesar, 1599.

As You Like It, circa 1599–1600.

Hamlet, circa 1600–1601.

The Phoenix and the Turtle, 1601.

Twelfth Night, circa 1601–1602.

Troilus and Cressida, 1601–02.

All's Well That Ends Well, 1602–1603.

Measure for Measure, 1604.

Othello, 1604.

King Lear, 1606.

Timon of Athens, 1605–1608.

Macbeth, 1606.

Anthony and Cleopatra, 1606–1607.

Pericles, circa 1607–1608.

Coriolanus, circa 1607–1608.

Cymbeline, 1609.

Sonnets, 1609.

The Winter's Tale, 1611.

The Tempest, 1611.

Cardenio, circa 1612–1613.

Henry VIII, 1613.

The Two Noble Kinsmen, 1613.

*   Dates by production

Annotated Bibliography

Andrews, John F. ed. *Romeo and Juliet: Critical Essays*. New York and London: Garland Publishing, Inc., 1993, 425p.

This collection of major essays on *Romeo and Juliet*, first printed in 1993, covers language, structure, performance, and Elizabethan culture. Editor John F. Andrews insures the essays are scholarly, yet readable. Included in this collection are strong essays by M.M. Mahood and Stanley Wells.

Davis, Lloyd. "'Death-Marked Love': Desire and Presence in Romeo and Juliet." *Shakespeare Survey* 49 (1996): 57–67.

Included in various volumes analyzing Shakespeare's *Romeo and Juliet*, Davis's essay explores how the events of the play lead to the ultimate tragedy. Davis puts particular emphasis on the darkness and deceit that is connected with desire and love.

Evans, Robert O. *The Osier Cage: Rhetorical Devices in Romeo and Juliet*. Lexington, Kentucky: University of Kentucky Press, 1966, 108p.

In his introduction, Evans states the purpose of *The Osier Cage* is to show how Shakespeare uses rhetorical devices in *Romeo and Juliet* to further his development of both plot and character. *The Osier Cage* focuses on the rhetoric of oxymora and the contradictions of human experience as they are presented in *Romeo and Juliet*.

Goldberg, Jonathan. *Shakespeare's Hand*. Minneapolis: University of Minnesota Press, 2003, 371 p.

Shakespeare's Hand provides a set of inquiries into the production, critical reception, and conditions of Shakespearean texts. Put together as a collection of essays, this volume offers a sustained, energetic, and rigorous study of the instability of Shakespearean texts and historical instability of the construction of gender, with particular attention paid to *Romeo and Juliet*.

Hamilton, Sharon. *Shakespeare's Daughters.* Jefferson, N.C.: McFarland, 2003, 184 p.

In an inclusive study of the father/daughter relationships that abound in Shakespeare's plays, *Shakespeare's Daughters* is a highly accessible companion to the study of the comedies, tragedies, and romances in Shakespeare's works. Within, Hamilton discusses Capulet's ineptitude as a father in *Romeo and Juliet.*

Hunt, Maurice, editor. *Approaches to Teaching Shakespeare's* Romeo and Juliet. New York: Modern Language Association of America, 2000, 219 p.

Hunt's book is a collection of valuable essays, combined to form a practical handbook for teachers and students which includes evaluations of film versions of *Romeo and Juliet*, background readings, and suggestions for classroom exercises.

Kristeva, Julia. *"Romeo and Juliet:* Love-Hatred in the Couple." *Tales of Love.* Trans. Leon S. Roudiez. Columbia UP, 1987. 209–233.

Using *Romeo and Juliet*, Kristeva seeks to illustrate her psychoanalytic theories that love is hate and vice versa. She explores the conflict between the passion of forbidden love and the repression of passion necessary for domesticated love.

Levenson, Jill. "Changing Images of *Romeo and Juliet:* Renaissance to Modern," in Habicht, Werner (ed.), Palmer, D.J. (ed.), Pringle, Roger (ed.), *Images of Shakespeare* Newark: University of Delaware Press, 1988, pp. 151–162.

In this essay, Levenson looks at the verbal constructs Shakespeare employs to differentiate the voices of Romeo and Juliet from the rest of the characters in the play. Additionally, she traces the way the characters of Romeo and Juliet have been seen from 1600 through 1999.

Levenson, Jill. *"Romeo and Juliet* before Shakespeare," *Studies in Philology* 81, no. 3 (1984 Summer): pp. 325–347.

This useful essay by Levenson provides a thorough discussion of Shakespeare's sources.

Lucking, David. "Uncomfortable Time in Romeo and Juliet." *English Studies: A Journal of English Language and Literature* 82, no. 2 (2001 April): p. 115–26.

Lucking looks at the relationship time to love and amatory rhetoric, as well as fate and the immortality of art.

Mahood, M.M. "*Romeo and Juliet*. Shakespeare's Wordplay." London: Methuen, 1957. 56–72. Rptd. in Romeo and Juliet: Critical Essays. Ed. John F. Andrews. New York: Garland, 1993. 55–71.

In this essay Mahood argues that the language of the play both connects us to and distances us from the events of the play. Shakespeare uses several poetic means in *Romeo and Juliet* such as paradox, recurrent image, and juxtaposition of old and young, with which to do so, ensuring that his readers have mixed emotions at the ending of the play.

Rabkin, Norman. "Eros and Death." *Shakespeare and the Common Understanding*. New York: Free Press, 1967.

Rabkin explores the paradox that Shakespeare promotes in *Romeo and Juliet*, that love is only fulfilled in death and that this is the basis of the tragedy. He asserts that Romeo and Juliet's hesitation makes them admirable, but that their lack of constraint also proves fatal.

Spurgeon, Caroline F.E. *Shakespeare's Imagery, and What it Tells Us*. Cambridge: Cambridge UP, 1935. pp. 310–316.

Spurgeon outlines the visual images, themes, and motifs that run through all of Shakespeare's plays. She also categorizes and compares everything in different ways, including comparisons with contemporaries like Marlowe, Jonson, and Bacon. Particularly she examines the significance of light imagery in *Romeo and Juliet*.

Wells, Robin. "Neo-Petrarchan Kitsch in *Romeo and Juliet*" *Modern Language Review* 93, No. 4 (1998 Oct): pp. 913–33

Explores the influence of the Petrarchan sensibility in Romeo's poetry and how Shakespeare satirizes it.

Wells, Stanley. "Juliet's Nurse: The Uses of Inconsequentiality." *Shakespeare's Styles*. Philip Edwards, Inga-Stina Ewbank, and G.K. Hunter, eds. Cambridge: Cambridge U P, 1980. 51–66. Reprinted. in *Romeo and Juliet: Critical Essays*. John F. Andrews, ed. New York: Garland, 1993. 197–214

Wells's essay concerns Juliet's nurses's famous speech in act 1, scene 3. His interest lies both in the speech's function within the play despite its seeming irrelevance, as well as its place in the development of Shakespeare's powers as a dramatist.

Contributors

Harold Bloom is Sterling Professor of the Humanities at Yale University. He is the author of over 20 books, including *Shelley's Mythmaking* (1959), *The Visionary Company* (1961), *Blake's Apocalypse* (1963), *Yeats* (1970), *A Map of Misreading* (1975), *Kabbalah and Criticism* (1975), *Agon: Toward a Theory of Revisionism* (1982), *The American Religion* (1992), *The Western Canon* (1994), and *Omens of Millennium: The Gnosis of Angels, Dreams, and Resurrection* (1996). *The Anxiety of Influence* (1973) sets forth Professor Bloom's provocative theory of the literary relationships between the great writers and their predecessors. His most recent books include *Shakespeare: The Invention of the Human* (1998), a 1998 National Book Award finalist, *How to Read and Why* (2000), *Genius: A Mosaic of One Hundred Exemplary Creative Minds* (2002), *Hamlet: Poem Unlimited* (2003), and *Where Shall Wisdom be Found* (2004). In 1999, Professor Bloom received the prestigious American Academy of Arts and Letters Gold Medal for Criticism, and in 2002 he received the Catalonia International Prize.

Neil Heims has published essays on Albert Camus, John Milton, and Virginia Woolf. He has also published a biography of J.R.R. Tolkien.

James C. Bryant is the author of *Tudor Drama and Religious Controversy*.

Gerry Brenner is a professor of English at the University of Montana. He has written several books on Earnest Hemingway. He has also published articles on a number of British and American authors including Scott Fitzgerald, Robert Browning, Jane Austen, Frank O'Connor, John Updike, and Geoffrey Chaucer.

Rudolf Stamm was the Associate Editor of *English Studies* from 1967 to 1986. He is the author of numerous articles and reviews on English and American drama.

Susanna Greer Fein teaches English at Kent State University.

François Laroque is Professor of English at the University of Paris. He is author of *Shakespeare's Festive World*.

Jerzy Limon is Professor of English Studies at the University of Gdansk, Poland, and the author of *Gentlemen of the Company: English Players in Central and Eastern Europe* and of *The Masque of Stuart Culture*.

Martin Goldstein's essay "The Tragedy of Old Capulet: A Patriarchal Reading of *Romeo and Juliet*" appeared in volume 77 of the journal *English Studies*.

Joseph A. Porter is Professor of English and Associate Chair of the English Department at Duke University. He is, the author of *The Drama of Speech Acts, Shakespeare's Mercutio*, and *Shakespearean Moorings*. He is the editor of *Critical Essays on Shakespeare's Romeo and Juliet*, the co-editor of the eight volume, *Renaissance Papers* and Editor-in-Chief of the *New Variorum Othello*. He has published a number of books of fiction under the name of Joe Ashby Porter.

Jill L. Levenson teaches in the Department of English, Trinity College, University of Toronto and is a Fellow of the Royal Society of Canada. She was President of the Shakespeare Association of America (1991–2), Chair of the International Shakespeare Association (2001), and the recipient of a Special Certificate of Merit for a career of distinguished service as an editor (1986).

Barbara Everett is a fellow of Somerville College, Oxford, and has also taught at Cambridge University and the University of

Hull. Among her works are *Poets in Their Time: Essays on English Poetry from Donne to Larkin*, and *Young Hamlet: Essays on Shakespeare's Tragedies*.

Acknowledgments

"The Problematic Friar in Romeo and Juliet" by James C. Bryant. From *English Studies*, 55, © 1974 by *English Studies*. Pp. 322–323, 328–329, 332–333. Reprinted by permission of Taylor and Francis, Ltd.

"Shakespeare's Politically Ambitious Friar" by Gerry Brenner. From *Shakespeare Studies: An Annual Gathering of Research, Criticism, and Reviews* XIII, ed. J. Leeds Barroll III, © 1980 by The Council for Research in the Renaissance. Pp. 47–48, 51–54, 56–57. Reprinted with permission.

"The First Meeting of the Lovers in Shakespeare's Romeo and Juliet" by Rudolf Stamm. From *English Studies*, 67(1), © 1986 by *English Studies*. Pp. 2, 5–11. Reprinted by permission of Taylor and Francis, Ltd.

"Verona's Summer Flower: The 'Virtues' of Herb Paris in Romeo and Juliet" by Susanna Greer Fein. From *ANQ: A Quarterly Journal of Short Articles, Notes, and Reviews*, 8(4), Fall 1995, © 1995 by Heldref Publications. Pp. 5–7. Reprinted with permission of the Helen Dwight Reid Educational Foundation.

"Tradition and Subversion in Romeo and Juliet" by François Laroque. From *Shakespeare's Romeo and Juliet: Texts, Contexts, and Interpretation*, ed. Jay L. Halio, © 1995 by Associated University Presses. Pp. 18–19, 23, 29–33. Reprinted with permission.

"Rehabilitating Tybalt" by Jerzy Limon. From *Shakespeare's Romeo and Juliet: Texts, Contexts, and Interpretation*, ed. Jay L. Halio, © 1995 by Associated University Presses. Pp. 101–105. Reprinted with permission.

Index